YOUR MIND CAN HEAL YOU

The soul contains the event that
shall befall it, for the event is only
the actualization of its thoughts.

*   *   *

The world is nothing; the man is all;
in *yourself* is the law of all nature . . . ;
in *yourself* slumbers the whole of Reason;
it is for you to know all; it is for you
to dare all.

*   *   *

The foundations of man are not in
matter, but in spirit.

*   *   *

. . . who can set limits to the remedial
force of spirit?

*   *   *

Who can set bounds to the possibilities
of man? . . . man has access to the entire
Mind of the Creator, is himself the creator
in the finite.

*   *   *

Place yourself in the middle of the
stream of power and wisdom which animates
all whom it floats, and you are without
effort impelled to truth, to right, and a
perfect contentment.

—RALPH WALDO EMERSON

YOUR MIND
CAN HEAL YOU

REVISED EDITION

by Frederick Bailes

DeVORSS & CO. INC.
P. O. BOX 550
MARINA DEL REY, CA 90294-0550

ISBN 0-87516-201-0
Library of Congress Catalog Card Number: 78-128864

Printed in the United States of America

To Mati

Contents

A Word to the Reader

Any person can have good health if he goes about it in the right way. Good health is not the gift of a whimsical Providence to a favored few. Sickness is not visited upon certain persons because an inscrutable Providence wishes them to "carry their cross" and thus achieve some nebulous spiritual purification. Health is the intended state for man and can be achieved.

In medical science, the first law of healing is: *Remove the cause.* That cause has usually been sought in the body tissues. Today, however, even medical practitioners have come to see that the fundamental cause of most sickness lies in the mind. This does not mean that people just imagine they are sick, and can then imagine they become well. The explanation lies far deeper than this in the intricate, complex activities of the human mind.

The real cause of sickness is found in tangled emotions, in the fears and anxieties, the jealousies and envies, the frustrations and bafflements, engendered by the attempts of men and women to achieve happiness and to meet the demands of modern life. Childhood impressions and teachings may be contributory causes. The impact of the myriad minds that surround them has a determining influence. The conversation of friends and relatives affects them. Added to these causes are the recital of symptoms and the instillation of fear that characterize the advertising of proprietary medicines.

The health warnings issued from time to time by insurance companies, health officers, and others who are seeking to safeguard the health of the public too often succeed only in implanting dread in the mind and have the effect of creating a fear-consciousness. This is not always a conscious thing upon the part of the recipient; usually it is entirely unconscious. The net effect is to build up in the minds of the people a great subjective body of fear-thought that affects the human organism day and night, asleep and awake, even though the one so affected may be entirely unaware of it.

In addition, the observation of certain illnesses in friends and relatives may create a state of fear and an apprehensiveness lest a similar condition attack the observer. The fact that parents or other relatives have suffered from certain disorders leads to the fear that perhaps there is a family tendency inherited by other members.

Whatever the basic fear-pattern, the fact remains that the real illness is not so much the outward physical manifestation as the underlying mental state. Illness is the outward sign of some inner mental or emotional disturbance. It follows that any remedial action directed *only* at the physical form will leave the fundamental cause untouched. In following the dictum *Remove the Cause,* the health-seeker must therefore learn *how* to erase the destructive thought-pattern before he can hope to eradicate the physical trouble.

The purpose of this book is to set forth, in everyday language, the way in which sickness stems from the thought-life and the exact method to be employed by the person who wishes to retrace his mental footsteps into complete freedom from the fear of sickness as well as from its actual form.

Since this information is for the layman, technical terms are avoided except where the meaning would be obscured by their omission. The indulgence of the scientifically trained reader is asked if at times scientific processes are explained in rather homely terms and by use of "unscientific" illustrations. After all, this book is intended to lead average, everyday readers into a clear understanding of universal forces that they may use in freeing themselves from sickness.

In a book of this nature, repetition is unavoidable since the same thought must be applied in diverse situations.

You have my very best wishes as you practice the principles outlined in this book. Tremendous forces—*waiting to move into action and bring you into radiant health*—lie within you.

FREDERICK BAILES

YOUR MIND CAN HEAL YOU

How Thought Causes Illness

> Man is not a body containing a mind; he is a mind operating through a body.

Man lives in his inner consciousness, not out in the outer world. He does not know that he has bumped into a material obstruction until the message has been carried through his nerves into his consciousness.

Under an anesthetic, where his consciousness is submerged, he does not feel pain. In certain hypnotic states, where the mind is directed in an opposite direction, he does not feel pain. Under hypnotic influence, women have been brought through childbirth without feeling the slightest distress. Patients have even been brought through surgery under such influence.

The things that man suffers, he suffers within his consciousness as his nerves report sensation.

HOW WE KNOW MENTAL STATES CAUSE ILLNESS

One must understand the true relation of mind to body in order to see why the assertion is made that mental states are responsible for illness. Man is not a body containing a mind; he is a mind operating through a body. This is a fundamental truth that must be accepted if there is to be mental and spiritual healing. The body of itself is the result of the activity of Mind, is molded by Mind, and changed by Mind.

Observation of superficial physical changes: Physical changes of a superficial nature can be observed following changed mental states. It seems scarcely necessary to mention that a sudden sense of shame causes the face to flush, and that fear causes it to turn pale.

The scientist explains the technical procedure in such instances by saying that the dilation and the contraction of blood vessels are under the control of the vasomotor nerves, which in turn are under emotional influence.

Scientific research and observations: Dr. Walter B. Cannon, of Harvard, was a pioneer more than fifty years ago in scientific research on the effect of emotions on the body.

During the last thirty to thirty-five years, exceedingly detailed and painstaking research and observations have been carried on in the medical schools of great universities, in hospitals, clinics, and medical centers, to determine the connection between the emotions and bodily conditions; and the results have been published in many books and in periodicals. The two studies very briefly summarized below were written up in much detail in *Psychosomatic Medi-*

cine, Journal of the American Psychosomatic Society, during the past year.

Upper respiratory infection was the subject of a study at Boston University School of Medicine.[1] Twenty-nine undergraduate students who had gone to the college health service within the past two weeks for treatment for severe upper respiratory infection were compared with twenty-nine students selected at random who had not had any such symptoms for at least a year and who had no history of major disorders.

Questionnaires and tests determined the following: the number of distressing life situations they had had during the previous year, the way they had dealt with those situations, and the effect on their emotions.

The group with the infections was found to have had "significantly more disappointment, failure, and role crisis" than the group with the good health record; in fact, personal disappointment, failures, and setbacks, uncertainty and indecision, had been building up over the year just past. They failed to deal satisfactorily with those distressing situations, the general reaction pattern being defiance; that is, rebelliousness, striking out against authority, retaliation, danger-seeking. The failure thus to resolve those situations resulted in a feeling of helplessness and the heightening of all unpleasant emotions, specifically in "more depression, hostility, and anxiety."

These reactions to the distressing situations, the study hypothesizes, weakens the body's natural defenses and makes it more susceptible to illness.

[1] Martin A. Jacobs, *et al.,* "Relationship of Life Change, Maladaptive Aggression, and Upper Respiratory Infection in Male College Students," *Psychosomatic Medicine,* January-February, 1969, pp. 31-44.

Asthma in children has been shown in a number of studies to be related to the psychological environment of the home.[2] Forty years ago, one such study found "great improvement" in twenty-three of twenty-five children who were away from home for from two months to more than a year, and no improvement in sixteen others remaining at home.

The Children's Asthma Research Institute and Hospital, of Denver, Colorado, studied twenty-five children with chronic asthma to find the effect of changing the psychological environment and keeping the physical environment the same by having their families leave the home and the children remain in it with a substitute parent.

Thirteen children, in whom the emotions of "anger, anxiety, excitement, depression" had been named by the parents as the important precipitating factors, showed, as a group, "a statistically significant decrease in symptoms" in all four ways by which the severity of the asthma was measured, and "an increase in symptoms on the family's return." The other twelve, in whom emotions had not been named as important precipitating factors, showed, as a group, improvement in one of the four measurements.

Dr. Charles Wahl, associate professor of psychiatry at the University of California at Los Angeles, says that psychic, or mental, stress may cause muscle tension that may contribute to rheumatoid arthritis because of the increased pressure on joints, or to low blood sugar because of the increased use of sugar in muscular contraction, or to hyper-

2 Kenneth Purcell, *et al.*, "The Effect on Asthma in Children of Experimental Separation from the Family," *Psychosomatic Medicine*, March-April, 1969, pp. 144-64.

ventilation, or to chronic low back pain, or to severe neck pains.

Dr. Margaret I. Sellers, an expert on viruses, also of the University of California at Los Angeles, says that anger, anxiety, and other emotional stresses may make it possible for virus infection, including that of polio, to enter the brain more easily. Such emotions release two body chemicals, adrenalin and serotonin, which help break down the body's strong natural defenses.

Stomach ulcers, skin disorders, heart trouble, anemia, digestive disturbances, colds, sinus trouble, polyps in the nose, colitis, and many other physical troubles have been scientifically traced to a mental origin.

HOW IT CAN BE THAT MIND HAS SUCH POWER

How can it be that the mind thus has such power to influence bodily states, even going so far as to develop actual disease conditions?

Man thinks with his whole body: It is because man thinks, not alone with his brain, but with his whole body. Every separate tiny cell is an infinitesimal spark of Mind. There is not a single point in the entire universe that is not indwelt by Mind; therefore, there is not a single atom in the body that is at any moment separated from mental action.

Man is so accustomed to think of two worlds—the physical and the mental—that he finds it hard to conceive of them both being one. Mental activity cannot be divorced from physical manifestation, for physical manifestation *is* mental manifestation. In a sense, that which the mind thinks, the body thinks; that which the body thinks, it becomes. Every varying mental condition records itself in the body; and as the mind changes, there is a corresponding change in the body, an exact reflection of the changed thought.

Illness is distorted thought in a visible state: Illness is some distorted idea that has assumed dominance. In the truest sense, it is incorrect to say that illness is "caused by" the mind. The distorted physical form that we call "illness" is the distorted thought-form in a visible state. The problem is primarily one of thought, and the solution is likewise. The control of sickness is mental, because sickness itself is mental.

The body of itself has no power to generate illness; illness is merely the shadow thrown by the mind. A healthy mind will shadow forth a healthy body; an unhealthy mind will shadow forth an unhealthy body.

Every new cell created in the body is either a negative or a positive thought in form. In the older days, it was customary to say that the cells are built "under the influence" of either negative or positive thought. In reality, the cells *are* the thought itself. Healthy thoughts mean healthy cells; sick thoughts mean sick cells. It is necessary to be very sure of this if one is to produce a bodily condition of abundant health.

When we consider that body cells are created as fast as lightning, we can understand how they are thought in form. As a simple example, the red corpuscles in the blood are built at the rate of approximately 1,000,000 a second, and normally are passing on at the same rate. Multiply this by the various other parts of the body, and one can readily see that this organism that we call "man" is a whirling dynamo of thought-energy, mind ceaselessly falling into form.

This being so, it is not at all farfetched to say that the control of sickness lies in the control of the thought, and that to change a physical condition one must change the thought. We therefore seek a technique that will enable us to change the character of the stream of consciousness. We shall come to this in a later chapter.

It is sufficient at this stage to say that the technique does not consist in will power, "concentration," or the repetition of "Day by day, in every way, I am getting better and better."

It consists in the conscious unification of oneself with Universal Intelligence, which never of itself has a sickness thought, therefore can never have a sickness form. There is a very definite technique by which the reader can lead himself into this unification.

Sickness is the outer evidence and sign of an inward disturbance. Health is the outward sign of an integrated mind.

EVIDENCES OF THOUGHT IN FORM

An evidence of thought in form is seen in the prank of the schoolboy who sucks on half a lemon in sight of his chum who is reciting on the platform. The resultant flow of saliva in the chum is purely mental in cause.

Dr. Arthur L. Bloomfield, of Stanford University Medical School, went a step further. He used twelve people in carefully safeguarded tests to determine the effect of mental action upon their digestive activities. These experiments had nothing whatever to do with the flow of saliva in the mouth, which is well established. They had as their object the determination of the amount of change, if any, in the flow of the digestive juices in the stomach.

To make sure that only the mental factor caused the change, the subjects were not allowed to see or smell food. They were placed in a room, and allowed to talk about their favorite foods or the preparation of them. The digestive juices in the stomach were collected and measured before and after the experiment. In two of the subjects, ten minutes' talking of delicious dishes had increased the digestive fluids six hundred per cent. In others, the added secretion ranged from one hundred per cent to lesser amounts.

This experiment is cited to show that it is not necessary to think of the particular manifestation in order to get it. Frequently, people will object that they were "not thinking of heart trouble" but they got it just the same. The subjects in the experiment were not asked to think about the flow of digestive fluids; they were told to talk and think about delicious foods. Consciously they thought of tasty food; subconsciously they produced a different effect, that of increased digestive flow, something allied to, but not exactly the same as, that of which they were thinking.

The conscious knowledge of these people may have been very limited as to the process of digestion. They may not have known that digestive fluids flow at the thought of food, nor even very much about the existence of such fluids at all.

But Universal Mind knows the entire process, for it originated it and builds in every foetus before birth the necessary structures to carry it out. In the next chapter, we shall show that the individual subjective mind is in reality the Universal Subjective Mind individually used. There is only One Mind, which acts under our conscious thinking in some functions, and independently of our conscious thought in others. This Mind governs the digestive processes; it has complete understanding of the connection between thoughts of food and the flow of digestive fluid, and proceeds to create accordingly.

Nothing comes into our life but what we attract: Nothing has ever come into our life but what we have asked for. Perhaps we should state it a little differently although the meaning is the same when one goes deeply enough beneath the surface. We could say that nothing has ever come into our life but what we have *attracted.* Now to reconcile these two ways of stating the same thing.

"I had not been thinking of arthritis": A man suffering from very severe arthritis came to see me following one of my church services. In response to something I said, he raised the objection that he "had not been thinking of arthritis but got it just the same."

The subsequent discussion brought out that his wife's sister lived about a mile away in the same city. He detested his sister-in-law and her husband, but his wife insisted upon their walking there every Sunday afternoon. He had tried every subterfuge to evade these weekly visits, but they had gone on for some years since his wife was an extremely strong-willed woman.

This inner conflict and his hidden rage, plus his very strong desire to find a way out of going, became the domi-

nant thought-pattern until it had become a controlling
factor.

After about twelve years of this, he began to develop
arthritis. It was a very gradual process, and finally he could
not take the weekly walks. They had no car; so he stayed
at home. He underwent all sorts of treatment, including
tonsillectomy and the extraction of his teeth, but for years
the arthritis persisted.

I pointed out to him the possibility that his mental experience had a direct connection with his physical condition, and that his desire not to walk to his relatives' home
had been taken up by Universal Mind so that he had attracted this physical condition—even asked for it. I showed
him how to adjust himself to the situation so as to remove
all sense of irritation from himself regarding it, and in two
months the arthritis had disappeared. His mind had healed
him.

UNIVERSAL MIND—IMPERSONAL LAW

Someone might say, "I would hate to have a God who
would give a man arthritis just because he hated going to
the home of loathed relatives." That is a hasty conclusion
and a faulty one.

In the next chapter, we shall show that Universal Mind
is entirely neutral. It has no personal desire; it works
through an impersonal Law. It knows the connection between swollen joints and inability to walk. It is directed
into action by our spoken or unspoken desire if this is
strong and clear enough to become dominant. Spirit is personal, but the Law is impersonal.

There is the Law of Thought, just as there is the law of electricity. The law of electricity will unemotionally and impersonally kill the person who grasps a naked power wire just as readily as it will toast his bread, because it knows nothing but to work according to the law of its action.

Man's ignorance makes it seem cruel: It takes thought and deep consideration to separate the activity of the Universal into its various phases—to know that God-Mind works strictly according to the Law of its being even when our ignorance makes us bring suffering to ourselves through its inexorable working.

Man is a newcomer to the universe. It is his business to make himself acquainted with the laws by which the universe in which he lives operates. He will suffer until he does. The child will suffer the cat's scratches until he learns that he must not pull the cat's tail. The same beneficent law of gravity that keeps the child from flying away from this planet out into space will kill him if he leans too far out of an upstairs window.

Law always seems cruel to him who does not understand it, and who in consequence runs counter to it. All natural laws are our masters as long as we do not understand them; when we understand them, they become our servants.

Just as the one who grasps the naked wire is unknowingly asking for or attracting death because he is doing a thing that in a universe of law cannot bring him anything but death, so the one who allows himself to be saturated with destructive thought is attracting destructive physical manifestation.

On the other hand, knowing the strict impersonalness of

the Law of Mind, he can swing into co-operation with it from the constructive side, and begin to experience the beneficent side of Law.

God is not unjust. In a sense, He says, "I have set before you life and death, blessing and cursing. Choose ye." In man lies the *power of choice* which can remake his personal world.

The very same Law of Mind that makes a man sick will make him well. Sickness is not a punishment for sin. With God there is no punishment. Sickness is the *consequence* of a wrong understanding and use of the Law of Mind just as a broken fishing pole is the result of a wrong understanding and use of the laws that pertain to tensile strength, or a crashing airplane is the result of a wrong application of the laws of aerodynamics. The personal element between God and man does not enter in at all in the sense of condemnation or punishment.

So the argument that God is cruel to cause sickness as a result of frustrations is incorrect reasoning, for as truly as the proper observance of the laws of aerodynamics will lift a man into the air and carry him easily to his destination, so will the Law of Mind lift and carry man into a high level of living, free from sickness and rejoicing in life, when he understands it.

Chaos would result if any law could be suspended for a moment. The elements composing matter would flow together and fly apart without rhyme or reason, and the universe would destroy itself. Whether we like it or not, we must face the fact that we live in a universe of unchanging law.

Man's progress depends on his knowledge of law: Happiness results from a proper adjustment to universal laws, unhappiness from maladjustment to law.

—*physical:* Man's progress from the cave to the modern apartment has resulted from his discovery of physical law and his subsequent use of it. Since physical comfort has been man's most pressing need, the centuries have been devoted to achieving it. He has learned how to use law to offset the heat and cold of the seasons, to ensure a full and varied supply of foodstuffs, to clothe himself properly, and to provide more rapid transportation than his legs could furnish.

Through the science of chemistry and physics, he is delving into the structure of matter, and is discovering laws pertaining to matter that are making life even more easy and comfortable.

It is a far cry from the caveman shivering in his cave in the bleak winters of antiquity to modern man with a steam-heated and air-conditioned apartment. If one had dared raise his voice in prehistoric days to venture the prediction that his destiny was the comfort and luxury of twentieth-century civilization, he would have been howled down, so difficult it is for the average mind to picture a freedom that he does not enjoy at the moment. The mastery of material law has, however, brought man to this new freedom.

—*mental and spiritual:* But man is primarily a thinker, and can never be content with mere animal comfort. Now the voice of the thinker is being heard. He is recognizing that his mental world is governed by law just as truly as his physical world is, and he is making serious efforts to uncover and use Mental Law. Just as he found to his delight that the proper use of physical law has increased his physical comfort, so he is finding that the proper use of Mental Law multiplies his mental and spiritual comfort.

The mastery of the Law of Mind will bring man the greatest liberation he has ever known. The physical benefits he has so far achieved are as nothing to the benefits he is on the verge of receiving as his researches delve deeper into all the ramifications of Mental Law. He will eradicate disease, abolish war and oppression of all sorts, and will find within himself a peace and happiness that he has never known.

To the skeptics, unable to accept anything that they have not as yet experienced, we would say, "Remember the caveman."

Even though mankind as a whole is not yet enjoying the full benefits of Mental Law, millions of individuals are finding increasing mastery in living, in deliverance from sickness, and in financial supply through their individual use of Law. The Australian aborigines might not believe that there is any such luxury as millions of people enjoy; yet that same luxury is available to every one who can achieve it.

So could every person today who still suffers under the darkness of a false belief in the inevitability of illness step out into freedom from sickness of all kinds as millions are doing, but he can never step out as long as he denies the possibility of this freedom. Meanwhile, he sits and hugs his sickness-belief closer to his bosom while others are using the Law of Mind to emancipate them from the belief in, and the distress of, sickness.

The world has been long in awaking to the fact that Mental Law contains man's happiness much more than does physical law. One would be unbalanced who would try to deny the marvelous blessings flowing from the discovery of the laws of physics, chemistry, and the other physical sciences. But we repeat that these blessings fade into insignificance in the presence of the gigantic possibilities of mental science.

THE HEALING MOVEMENT

A new day is dawning; in fact, the sun is well above the horizon. From earliest times there have been mental and spiritual healings and mental and spiritual practitioners. Before Moses lifted up his brazen serpent, occasional mental and spiritual healings were recorded.

Since then, never a century has passed without sporadic cases of direct healing being reported, often through men who did not think of themselves primarily as healers, but who carried a message of spiritual life.

(From time to time I use the term "healer," but let it be clearly understood that there is no "gift" of healing.)

In the religious field alone, John Wesley, Dwight L. Moody, John Alexander Dowie, A. B. Simpson, and others all saw the seeming miracle of men and women, who had formerly been held in spiritual slavery as well as in physical distress, receiving instantaneous physical healing as their mental state was changed in what was then called "conversion."

The healing movement has now assumed large proportions and is growing. From isolated, apparently accidental healings, it has developed into well-organized institutions over the world. Spiritual healing has long since passed the

state where it was contemptuously referred to as a "cult";
it is now the method of healing used by over fifteen million people in the United States today.

The principles of spiritual healing are now known; the
reasons why results are achieved are known; and the reasons for its apparent failure in isolated cases are also
known. The things that obstruct healing are known, and
the mental attitudes that produce healing are tabulated,
codified, classified, and systematized. Spiritual and mental
healing has passed from a "cult" to a science all within the
past one hundred years. Each year sees more and more
people accepting it, to their lifelong joy, and it is rolling
into popular acceptance like a gigantic snowball.

Growth by results: How has this method of treating sickness grown? By one thing alone. It has proved itself by its
results.

Consider the fact that it involves a revolutionary change
in one's accepted ideas of the origin of illness. The empha-
sis is steadily shifting from the physical, where it has pre-
dominantly been since early days, into the mental world.
It calls for less dependence on material methods and a
greater reliance upon the intangible power of thought. For
the pioneers, it called for a leap across a wide chasm; yet
those few daring souls who made the leap received results
that compelled observers to ponder.

Little by little, others somewhat gingerly experimented,
and to their delight they found that there was something
there after all. Anything that proves itself will gain adher-
ents, and thus, like a chain letter, every new healing brings
many more into acceptance of this rediscovered truth.

Where once the term "mental and spiritual healing" was

greeted with derisive laughter, it is now treated, even among the material scientists, with the respect it deserves. It is not easy to sneer at people who are now walking around in perfect health who once were given up to die of such diseases as cancer, diabetes, heart trouble, paralysis, to say nothing of so-called lesser troubles.

They who are healed may not always be able to explain just how it was done, but they have had a definite experience like the man in the story of Jesus who is reported to have said, "Who he is or how he did it, I do not know; but I do know that whereas once I was blind, now I can see." After all, results speak louder than explanations, and are immovable by argument.

The practice of mental and spiritual healing is coming more and more into its rightful place in our daily lives. The more progressive physicians are investigating it, and many are using it to a greater or a lesser degree with benefit to their patients. The physician of the future will try to correct the thought-life of his patient, thus treating the inner cause as well as the outer effect.

Truth as old as the universe: It is an old truth even though but recently rediscovered. It is as old as the universe because it is basic in the universe.

As one studies the material universe with unprejudiced eyes, he is forced to the conclusion that it must have been formed by the action of thought because matter has no power to originate itself. Like an underground continent whose mountains form the isolated islands of the ocean is this great fundamental truth whose isolated healings throughout history have attested its presence.

It is new only in its restatement and in its systematized

presentation. Known vaguely before, it is now known with very great exactness. We know beyond the shadow of a doubt that bodily conditions are the *reflection of mental states,* and can be changed without the intervention of any material means simply through changed thought.

Systems of nonmaterial healing: The different systems of nonmaterial healing are approaching the subject from different angles, but are converging upon the one point— that changed thought brings changed physical activity.

The psychologist and the psychiatrist are keeping their work upon the level of strictest mental performance, hesitating to introduce the spiritual element since they consider the religious approach outside their province.

We approach it with the assumption that it is a spiritual science since we have observed that most healings of this kind come from, or lead to, a new interest in spiritual questions. In consequence, we appeal to the spiritual nature of man, believing that his spiritual awakening is evidence of a spiritual perfection within, which, uncovered, leads to his healing.

This does not mean that this is a new religion. It is a spiritual awakening, but not a denominational one. This truth can be applied in any denomination without interfering with one's particular religious belief. There is only one God in the entire universe. Men may find their way to Him through the denominational channel of their own choosing. The important thing is that they reach Him and establish personal contact.

When a steamer leaves port, loved ones endeavor to maintain contact with the departing friends as long as possible. The streamers thrown from deck to pier may be yellow, red, blue, or any other color. The color is not important; the important thing is the contact thus established. It would be ridiculous for the one holding a blue streamer to say his neighbor's green one is of the wrong color so long as it leads from friend to friend.

So the important thing in life is to establish the direct contact with the Creator; the denominational color of the contacting medium means little. A gorgeous golden streamer that fails to reach from one to the other is not worth as much as a plain one that does.

The Principle of this science is the link that enables man to contact Reality. That Principle may be overlaid with any color of the rainbow because it can be laid hold of by any person of any denomination, any color, creed, or country. The Principle is universal.

We think that the approach of the psychologist is good as far as it goes, but weaker than ours because he recognizes the presence of many individual minds while we recognize only One Mind, which embraces all so-called individual minds. In following chapters, we shall see that once we have come to a conclusion regarding the eternal state of that One Mind, which eternally is peace, tranquillity, power, love, faith, harmony, expansion, health, and completeness, our objective is to bring what we call our individual mind into a state of oneness with the One Mind.

Thus, since Universal Mind is forever undisturbed by any hostile force, never recognizes the existence of anything unlike itself, then our mind, being of that One Mind, cannot experience anything not experienced in that Mind.

This indicates the difference between the systems of non-material healing, the explanation of which is often sought in the question, "Where does your method differ from that of psychology, psychiatry, psychoanalysis, and psychosomatic medicine?"

POINTS FOR SPECIAL CONSIDERATION

The reader who wants to discover man's true nature and begin to make practical application of what he has learned will think through each idea below very carefully, and will govern his thoughts accordingly.

Man lives in his inner consciousness, not out in the outer world.

Superficial physical changes can be observed following changed mental states.

Scientific research verifies one's own observations.

What the mind thinks, the body thinks; what the body thinks, it becomes.

Healthy thoughts mean healthy cells; sick thoughts mean sick cells.

Sickness is the outer evidence of an inward disturbance.
Health is the outer evidence of an integrated mind.

All natural laws are our masters as long as we do not understand them; when we understand them, they become our servants.

CHAPTER

II

The Reality and Scope of Mind

When one reaches an inner awareness that he is indwelt by all the Power and Presence of God, not just a tiny fragment of it, it awakens within him a sense of security never before imagined possible.

This chapter gives further facts upon which we base our assurance of healing, and lays the groundwork for a common understanding of the terms used. It is necessary that we define and understand our terms since the whole science of healing is based upon a proper understanding of the mind, the way it works, and its relation to the great Mind of the universe.

COSMIC INTELLIGENCE AT WORK

Thinking people are able to see clear evidence of a Cosmic Intelligence at work throughout the universe. Einstein declared that there is indisputable evidence of laws of order in the universe. In this he has been supported by Jeans, Eddington, Millikan, and other leading physicists.

Before we can agree that there is an Intelligence back of the universe, we should have the right to ask, "Where is the evidence of this Intelligence?"

We see Intelligence working through law in the way particles of matter are drawn to, or repelled from, each other. The whole science of chemistry is based upon the undeviating working of this orderly Intelligence. Every blade of grass that grows follows an orderly plan. Every cell in a stalk of celery is built according to an intelligent plan. The location and movement of the stars and the planets evidence a guiding, creative Intelligence.

The various organisms that exist upon our planet, from the tiniest microbe to the largest elephant, show in the construction of their bodies an intelligent plan that unfolds as it builds exact structures to do exact work. It is no accident that heart, stomach, nerves, and blood vessels are constructed as they are, and that within each species they are always constructed alike.

MAN'S RELATION TO COSMIC INTELLIGENCE

If we can agree that there is an Intelligence back of the universe, the next logical question is, "What is our relation to this Intelligence?"

If we can answer this, we can solve the problem of sickness, for at the beginning let it be said that the secret of healing lies in man's ability consciously to unite with this Universal Intelligence and to draw upon it for the removal of disease thought-patterns and the substitution of a health thought-pattern.

This is far easier to do than most people imagine. Millions of men and women have already done it and eliminated sickness from their experience. I see it done every day of my life by those with whom I am brought into contact.

But to return to the relationship of man to the Intelligence throughout the universe:

Science has found that all intelligence is one, just as it has discovered that all matter is one, and that all the so-called different laws of the universe are in reality One Law. The intelligence that man uses to spade his garden or to select and plant flowers is the same Intelligence that grows the flowers and runs the universe. *It differs in degree only, never in kind.* We may not understand this truth, but the fact remains that whenever we think, we think with the One Mind of the universe. It can truthfully be said that man's mind is God's Mind.

There is no such thing as "your" mind and "my" mind. That which we call "individual" mind is merely that much of Universal Mind as one is using at the time. There is no such thing as "my" air and "your" air; there is only one air equally distributed around our planet, and that which I call "mine" is merely that much of this surrounding air as I have drawn into my lungs for the moment. In another moment, it may be drawn into the lungs of someone else and become "his."

When we understand that the Universal Mind fills the universe, we can then picture it as a great surrounding ocean of Mind, in which we are submerged and upon which we draw.

THREE ASPECTS OF THE INFINITE THINKER

One aspect of this Mind seems to be subjective, or subconscious; that is, it seems to have no power of choice, but must be directed into action. It is highly intelligent, has all the knowledge of the universe within it, but it is not reasoning Mind. Its nature is to move in the direction to which it is directed.

The question might be asked as to who or what does the choosing, reasoning, and directing. This seems to be done by another phase of Infinite Intelligence that we might call First Cause, or Spirit.

If we go back, away beyond the beginning of anything that is formed, we are forced to the conclusion that the universe must have been thought formed. Science knows that the earth could not possibly have called itself into being. The chief property of matter is inertia; that is, it has no power to move itself in any particular. Matter must always be acted upon by some form of energy outside itself.

Every form of energy we know of in the universe is material in its source except one, and that is *thought*. Thought is the product of Intelligence; therefore, we can safely assume that before matter flowed into form there must have been an Intelligence that could cause this condensation into form. Some people call this Intelligence "God." Others call it "Cosmic Intelligence," "the Infinite Thinker," or simply "the Infinite." The name does not matter; the fact of its existence does.

This Intelligence operates in the two ways we have named: *first,* as a selective, originating Intelligence that determines what it wants done; *second,* as an obeying Intelligence, carrying out the directions of the originating Intelligence.

This second phase of the Intelligence operates always and entirely as law, having all the knowledge necessary to construct anything that is made, but working always with a pattern before it from which it is unable to deviate. If it were able to deviate, there would be no law in the universe, and chaos would result. In fact, there never could have been a universe in the first place, for unless two and two always make four, nothing can be built. As Sir James Jeans, distinguished astrophysicist, said:

The universe can best be pictured as consisting of pure thought, the thought of what for want of a better word we must describe as a mathematical Thinker.

Once we have arrived at the fact of God as the Intelligence of the universe, we can separate His activities or manifestations into three for the purpose of better understanding His method of operation.

At this juncture there should be no misunderstanding. God is indivisible and cannot possibly be separated into parts; therefore, this separation is entirely a matter of words so we can keep our finite thinking straight.

We have, then, the One Infinite Thinker operating in what we might call three planes, which we might explain by using a much overworked and misunderstood term, namely, "vibrations."

We have God as Spirit, the highest, least tangible vibration, wishing to create a formed universe. With Spirit, to wish is to create.

Within Spirit is the great Unformed Substance of the universe, which ultimately will become the formed universe, called by some "the Body of God." This Substance, characterized by inertia, must be acted upon by a force outside itself. It is of the lowest, most tangible vibration.

Spirit therefore uses Mind operating as Law to mold and form the universe into the dense material that we know. The vibration of Mind, being lower than that of Spirit, makes it subject to Spirit, and being higher than that of matter, makes matter subject to it; therefore, God as Mind might be termed the middle vibration. Thus Spirit, *First Phase,* speaks its will, and Mind, *Second Phase,* obeys unquestioningly, to mold Unformed Substance, *Third Phase,* into the form of the Pattern that Spirit holds.[1]

THREE ASPECTS OF THE HUMAN THINKER

Since man is in the small what God is in the large, man is a similar trinity. Man is material in his body, thus one with God on the lowest vibration. He has a subjective, or subconscious, mind, making him one with God on the second level. And he is a thinker, being one with God on the highest level of vibration.

Body: It is necessary, before going deeply into the *modus operandi* of healing, clearly to understand that the body of man is made of the great Unformed Substance, which is

[1] For a more detailed explanation of this creative activity, see Judge Thomas Troward's *The Creative Process in the Individual.*

the raw material of the universe, and which has been called the Body of God.

Man's body, therefore, is by no means a vile thing. It is a sacred temple in which Spirit dwells, and through which Spirit operates by the Law of Mind. True, man's body is of a lower vibration than Spirit or Mind, being more dense, but at the same time it is Spiritual Substance, and unless one clearly grasps this truth, he will miss much of the pre-requisite knowledge for healing.

Mind: The psychologist tells us that man's mentality is divided into two levels: not two minds, but two phases of one mind, variously called conscious, or objective, and sub-conscious, or subjective.

—conscious, or objective—its directive function: Man's conscious, or objective, mind is that phase of his mind of which he is most steadily conscious. When he awakes in the morning and looks at the clock, it reports the time to him. Through it, he *chooses* to take a certain route to work. Through it, he makes other conscious *choices* throughout the day.

It is *reasoning, choosing, directing* mind.

It corresponds to Spirit in the Infinite Thinker. By this we do not suggest that man's conscious thinking is perfect —we know it is sometimes devilish—but man is spirit in that he has the power of *reason* and *selection,* and the abil-ity to *direct* subjective mind into the channel that he *decides.*

—subconscious, or subjective: But when sleep comes at night, the conscious, or objective, mind stops choosing, and the mental activities of the sleeping hours are largely the

product of the subconscious, or subjective, mind, noticed chiefly in the creation of dreams.

It is that great, buried, unconscious depth in which are stored all the memories of his past thought and action, which are not gone even though he cannot consciously recall them, but which float up in dreams and complexes.

But man's subconscious mind is more than he has put into it, for it is one with the great surrounding ocean of Mind, which Ralph Waldo Emerson described clearly and beautifully when he called it the Over-Soul.

—subconscious, or subjective—its intelligence: The Universal Subjective Mind, with which man's subconscious, or subjective, mind is one, has infinite intelligence.

If we would pool all the skill, learning, and intelligence of all the scientific men in the world, there would not be enough to create and grow one fingernail on a finger; yet this Universal Subjective Mind knows exactly how to lay down cell after cell in millions of fingernails and make each one perfect, as it is doing at this moment. No one knows how to put the fragrance in a single flower; yet this Mind is touching millions of flowers daily with its magic wand, and distilling their subtle essences into perfume from the soil, water, air, and sunlight.

The Universal Subjective Mind knows how every successful business is built. It knows in exact detail just what is needed to turn ideas into cash. It knows how to take a sick business and make it well, or how to turn a defeated life into a masterpiece. It does not have to reason; it *knows.* Already it has the knowledge that man needs to lift him out of every limiting circumstance, and flood his life with good.

Man boasts of every tiny discovery he makes. The Universal Subjective Mind knows them all before he gropes his faltering way toward them.

This is the Mind with which man's subconscious mind is one.

—*subconscious, or subjective—its creativeness:* Man's subconscious, or subjective, mind is creative. It is that which carries on the multifarious activities of the body. Nothing goes on anywhere in the universe without Mind, and this includes the body.

Subconscious mind keeps the heart beating, the diaphragm falling and rising to bring air into, and expel it from, the lungs. It keeps all the digestive and eliminative processes going. It keeps the nerves carrying nerve energy to every inch of the body. It manufactures the fluids, hormones, and enzymes within the body. It keeps the temperature always at the proper degree through the burning of the correct amount of fuel and through the control of the heat-regulating apparatus.

It does all this and a great deal more, easily and effortlessly, as we shall show in a later chapter, carrying on operations that man's conscious intelligence does not know how to do. The reason it can do all this is that man's subconscious mind is in reality one with the Universal Subjective Mind.

When we understand that there is only One Mind in the entire universe, and that man is in and of that Mind, we can readily see that the Mind that made the body cells in the first place can just as easily make new cells stamped with the picture of life.

—*subconscious, or subjective—its obedience:* And when

we understand that the Universal Subjective Mind builds always according to the pattern laid down by Spirit, and that the whole Power of the universe awaits man's recognition of himself as spirit, privileged to speak the word that directs Mind to follow that pattern, it is easy to see that we can set the Law of Mind in motion in the direction that we desire.

This has been observed in such a small thing as awaking from sleep. Most people have had the experience of deciding to get up at a certain hour in the morning, perhaps an hour earlier than usual. This is a conscious choice, and at that very hour subjective mind has wakened them, often just two seconds before the alarm went off.

This is an example of what we mean by saying that man as spirit, or objective mind, has as a servant subjective mind, which *obeys* his conscious choices.

One of its most important characteristics is its absolutely neutral *obedience* to conscious mind. It has positively no wishes of its own, no preferences. It stands forever as the servant of conscious mind. But there is no compulsion here; there is equality.

It is similar to a happy home, in which each partner considers the other equal. The man goes out to earn the money; the woman stays at home to keep house. The man suggests that he would like chicken for dinner. It is not a command; such is the harmony between them that his wishes are hers. She—as an equal—accedes to his request without any sense of coercion. That is the work that she is fitted to do, and that she has accepted as her part of the bargain.

One of the difficult things for some people to grasp is

that Universal Mind, almighty with all the powers of the Infinite Thinker, is willing to be the servant of man and to flow into action in the direction that he chooses to indicate. They have been imbued with the idea that man is a worm of the dust, and God the Autocrat of the heavens; that it is unthinkable that all the Power and the Activity of God await their directing word, willing and ready to move into creative activity as they direct. Yet this is exactly what awaits them when they understand their privileges as incarnations of God.

Just so long as they hesitate and regard this Power with awe, they are left floundering in a morass. But it is a morass entirely of their own creation. The moment they accept their rightful place and send the Law into motion for themselves, they find that they are dealing with a Power which, while great enough to break them, is surrendered entirely to their will.

There must be no superstition and no awe in thus approaching this Healing Power. This mighty Healing Power is not a person; it is a Principle. It is the fundamental Principle in the universe. It is a natural law. It is impersonal. It has no more self-consciousness than the law of electricity. It is entirely neutral. It is ready at man's behest to grant its creative power.

We could imagine a Pygmy from Central Africa approaching an electric light switch for the first time with fear and awe; yet a child reared in a modern home knows that he has only to press the button to get light. The law of electricity is absolutely neutral. The child, the Pygmy, or the scientist can press the button, and the electricity flows in response. It has no wishes of its own. It will remain inactive until someone sets it into action, and it cares not who does it. Its nature is to move into action as someone performs the necessary acts. But the laws of its action must be observed: there must be tight connections, and it must be connected with the source of its power. That is all.

So in like manner does the Law of Mind respond to an intelligent use of its power. Its creative force is thrown in any direction one wishes, the only requirement being that the laws of its action be observed. It is sufficient to say at this time that one must keep in mind that there is, at this very moment, a flood of Universal Power dedicated to his use, awaiting his word, and entirely subservient to his will.

He does not have to pray to it, ask it, plead with it. He has merely to recognize it, and know within himself that it is his for the enlarging of his life, health, happiness, and prosperity.

But it never offers nor forces its services; it awaits recognition. This is the reason for one of the tragedies of life, for man has to discover for himself that he has a powerful ally ready and able to take him to the place where he wants to be; yet for all practical purposes it is not there until he discovers and uses it.

MAN'S JOURNEY OF SELF-DISCOVERY

Man is on a journey of self-discovery. The old theory that God takes pity on man, steps in and reveals Himself when man is at the end of his resources is no longer acceptable or tenable.

In the dim ages of antiquity, the guiding Intelligence of the universe took the forms of life just as far as each could go. From the slime of the primordial ocean-bed, the protozoon was indwelt by Intelligence, and as this organism acted upon that which it was able to sense, it developed a greater use of Intelligence. It could have been a man, but it did not know it. It was a protozoon, and as such it functioned, getting food, eliminating waste, and reproducing.

As the general creative scheme swept onward, this single-celled organism was able to use a slightly little more of that vast reservoir of Intelligence, and it developed by gradual stages, and over long periods of time, until it came to the place where it had *self-consciousness.* Its intelligent life up until now had been entirely subjective, drawing upon the great Universal Subjective Mind. But after millions of years it arrived at the stage of development where a peak of *objective* mind had been pushed up above the level of its subjectivity, and it was then a man, in the image and likeness of God. This image and likeness consists in man's *self-consciousness, reason,* and power of *choice.*

Man was now on his own, mentally speaking.

His access to unlimited Power: From this point, his further progress was dependent upon his recognizing his access to unlimited Power.

Some do not yet see this, and flounder around at the mercy of circumstances. Yet during their futile efforts to make headway, the same Infinite Intelligence is at their disposal if they only knew it. It will not force itself upon them; they must get their eyes open to it.

Many have come to the place where they see this truth, and for them a new life is dawning. They are moving out of the place of sickness and defeat into their intended place of health and mastery. Their numbers are increasing with every hour. This new knowledge is being increasingly accepted. Man can advance as rapidly as he can make himself acquainted with it.

There is no limit set by Infinite Mind. Man can go as far as he wishes, or stay where he is.

His responsibility to choose his destination: The only limiting factor is man himself. If he continues to sit and shiver in the cold, whimpering and complaining, that is his right as a free agent. But he can pick himself up and make his way to the warm glow of the eternal fire, and enter into a life that contains all the elements of happiness. Others can help him but cannot do it for him; even God cannot do it for him. It is his job and his alone. On his voyage of self-discovery, he is the captain of his ship, and therefore solely responsible for making harbor.

Man's responsibility, then, is to *choose* his destination; the motive power to bring him there is furnished by the Infinite.

Only when he grasps this fundamental fact will he be prepared to relinquish his own unaided efforts and to rely upon Cosmic Mind to keep the engines running while he steers the ship. Just as impersonally as a ship's engines respond to proper direction, so does the Universal Law of Mind respond to man's conscious direction.

THE UNLIMITED POWER TO WHICH MAN HAS ACCESS

We understand that we live in an ocean of Subjective Mind. That which surrounds us we call Universal Subjective Mind; that which we use of it we call individual subjective mind.

The more one is able to conceive of himself as using the Universal Mind, the more potent his thought becomes. The individual can increase to infinity his concept of the Power available for his use if he clears his vision and understanding sufficiently. He will always find that there is as much of the Power as he can mentally accept.

There need be no fear that he will ever reach the place where he will deplete the Universal. He could use *all* the Cosmic Power without reducing it one unit. Even if every living soul were sufficiently awakened so that all were drawing to the greatest extent upon the Universal, there would still be no diminution of that Power. The Power is infinite, limitless, inexhaustible, resistless.

Man lives in a world of the senses. He is bounded by his erroneous concepts of space and time. He applies quantitative terms to spiritual things, failing to see that God does not have size.

In fact, all of God fills the entire universe; yet all of God is in every man. Moreover, all of God is in each single cell of the body, in every tiny organism, in every blade of grass; yet there is no separation into pieces. God, being indivisible, is in every place with all of Himself at every and any moment. He is not cut up into trillions of tiny pieces in order to indwell the different organisms. We must rid ourselves of this material notion which is the result of material reasoning.

There is more to the foregoing than we might see at first. It is a fundamental that we should grasp, because when we first awake to its significance, it is a concept that staggers the imagination.

When one reaches an inner awareness of the fact that he

indwelt by all the Power and Presence of God, not just a tiny fragment of it, it awakens within him a sense of security never before imagined possible. When he glimpses the vastness of the truth that all the Universal Power flows through his body, he is able to sit back in quiet assurance with a total absence of fear at the appearance of illness, for his fear has been created by his picture of himself invaded by an enemy strong, cruel, and merciless. This is the reason why he has never been able to believe that his little mentality could possibly cope with this monster of illness.

But now he has a new picture. This illness is not any longer a towering creature. All things are relative. In the face of the Universal Healing Power and Presence, the disease-form pales into insignificance. It shrinks in his sight to a puny, undernourished apparition that is trying to scare him. He knows it for what it is—an ugly picture trying to assume reality.

He knows that the only Reality in the universe is Spirit; that the material world, with all its varying forms, is only the shadow world, while the real world is the world of Spirit and Mind. So he is freed from his lifelong fear of sickness, because "Greater is He that is for us than they that are against us."

The universe as a demonstration of its working: Man does not have to accept so-called revelation in order to know God. Unquestionably the sacred writings have told us much about Deity; but we do not have to accept their conclusions when they violate our reason, or when they conflict with what we ourselves are able to observe. After all, the sacred writings are not so much God's revelation to man; they are more truly the results of man's groping after

God. True, men of lofty vision and spiritual intuition penned them, and as such we should be thankful for their thought.

But it is not incumbent upon us to accept them *in toto* as final. We too have reason, judgment, and power of observation. The knowledge that we arrive at through our own mental processes is just as valid a revelation as that given to us by anyone who lived in the past.

Man can watch for himself the working of Intelligence in the universe, and thus build his own faith in this Universal Power and Intelligence. Thus he builds upon a foundation that he himself has laid rather than upon one that has been laid by another.

Consider the universe as a demonstration of the working of Intelligence. We know that the planet upon which we live is a weighty mass moving in an orderly path around the sun. Likewise, eight other known planets of varying sizes move on an exact time schedule around the sun, thus making up our solar system. Farther out in space other heavenly bodies move; in fact, our entire solar system is itself revolving about another star.

The sizes of these stars and planets, their distances from one another, are staggering to the imagination.

Our earth measures approximately 8,000 miles in diameter, but the sun is approximately 866,000 miles in diameter. And the sun is dwarfed by another star, Alpha Herculis, with a diameter of 650,000,000 miles, about 800 times that of the sun and more than 80,000 times that of the earth. Astronomers say that still larger stars may be found.

The sun is about 93,000,000 miles from the earth, a distance which is almost incomprehensible; yet the 200-inch telescope on Mt. Palomar shows a galaxy of stars 5,000,000,-000 *light-years* away. *One light-year* is approximately *6,000,000,000,000 miles.*

All this vast army of heavenly bodies marches through space like an army of soldiers, each one pursuing its trackless path through trillions of miles of space, each one exactly on time, as though guided by the invisible fingers of a Master Marionettist.

The invisible directing Agency is Cosmic Mind. It displays a high order of intelligence—Infinite Intelligence. It demonstrates limitless power. Tremendous energy must be exerted to move those massive bodies through space; yet it is done silently, surely, certainly by this Infinite Intelligence that must also be Infinite Power.

It is no wonder that a prominent astronomer is reported to have said that there are no atheists among astronomers.

This is the Intelligent Power to which man has access because *he is one with the Universal Mind.*

Just so long as he continues to remain blind to this fact, he will continue to live the life of a slave. That tremendous Power is available for his use, but it will not be called into use until he himself calls it. When he understands and accepts the fact that the same Power that holds the universe in action is ready to hold his body free from sickness, then he can know that there are no incurable diseases—only incurable people, incurable because they remain blind to their potential healing.

Those who think that their healing depends upon their

own puny mental efforts, such as concentration, will power, and so on, will be disappointed; but those who learn how to allow this Universal Intelligence to flow in their behalf will find liberation and healing.

This, then, is the Intelligence and the Power that man can send into action. Mighty as it is to hold a universe in harmony, it is obedient to the thought and the word of man, and can be directed toward the building of perfect health, happiness, and prosperity by that person who understands its complete responsiveness. This is the Law of Mind whose power we invoke. It is greater than anything that seems to oppose our desires.

Nothing in this universe has the power to frustrate us, because we are one with the God-Mind and God-Power. Let us arise and claim our birthright, for the reality of Mind is absolute and its scope limitless.

POINTS FOR SPECIAL CONSIDERATION

The reader who wants to discover man's true nature and learn how to use his understanding to help himself and his family will go through the chapter again, watching for everything on the following fundamentals, and will think them through from every point of view until he is very sure he has grasped them thoroughly.

Man's body is one with the Body of God.
It is a sacred temple in which Spirit dwells.

Man's subconscious, or subjective, mind is one with Universal
    Subjective Mind.

It has access to limitless Intelligence and Power to heal.

Man's conscious, or objective, mind is one with God as Spirit. It has the power to reason, weigh, and *choose*.

Man is indwelt by *all* the Power and the Presence of God.

III

The Universal Healing Principle

Beneath all methods of healing is a fundamental Healing Principle that is contacted whenever anyone gets well.

It is clearly evident that a Healing Principle, operating independently of any medication by man, exists in the universe.

A redwood—or any other tree for that matter—heals itself by forming what the tree surgeon calls a "burl" at the point where the limb has broken off. The burl is composed of brand-new cellular material that forms new thickened wood tissue and heals the stump.

A bird in the forest, breaking a wing or a leg, is healed after a lapse of time. The torn hide of a jungle animal heals without outside intervention.

A pin prick on man's finger does the same. Small cuts and bruises are likewise healed "by nature," as we say. In fact, in frontier days men who had sustained severe gunshot wounds or stabbings away out far from competent medical aid "holed up," as they called it, in some secluded place and eventually came out healed.

It is one of the wonders of nature that these bodies of ours, so fragile and easily injured, seem to possess within themselves something that tends to start a healing operation soon after injury occurs.

Yet in the past there has been intense rivalry among the various schools of healing on the human plane, each insisting that its alone was the true method, and that all others should be barred from practice. If the cure lies in the particular method employed, it would seem reasonable to expect that only that method would restore people to health, and that none of the others would ever be able to induce recovery in the patient.

But they all got people well; therefore, it occurs to thinking people that deep beneath the particular method used, *there must be something else* that really accomplishes the recovery of the patient, namely, a Universal Healing Principle.

HEALINGS AMONG EARLY MAN

Healings among early man were mental. Back in the early days of his existence, it was believed that sickness was due to the invasion of the body by evil spirits. The witch doctor gradually developed incantations designed to drive out those evil spirits. In some cases, this method proved efficacious; so he kept particular formulae in the body of his treatment and gradually added others that seemed to produce healing results.

Those early witch doctors were shrewd observers, and

began to note that certain herbs possessed medicinal prop-
erties. Powdered or brewed into an infusion, they could
be applied to the exterior of the body for the healing of
wounds and bruises, or taken internally for pains and other
distress.

Thus the witch doctor added incipient materia medica
to his incantations. Since this knowledge was valuable to
him, enabling him to wield tremendous influence in the
tribe, he guarded it jealously, allowing no one to pry into
the mystery of his treatment. As his sons grew up, he im-
parted his knowledge to the eldest, eventually to all of
them, keeping it strictly within the family and surrounding
it with an atmosphere of mystery.

As the centuries passed, this body of knowledge grew to
remarkable proportions in the hands of the witch doctors.
Eventually those who liked facts and objective realities,
who had what today might be called the scientific mind,
turned more and more to the herbal methods and less and
less to incantations. Those who were more alive to the
reality of the unseen world and to the play of less tangible
forces specialized more and more in the latter. Thus were
born the two great professions—medicine and the priest-
hood.

DIVERSE MATERIAL METHODS OF HEALING

The world is familiar with the tremendous advance that
the science of medicine has made. In the thousands of
years that have elapsed since the witch doctor, the men of
medicine have constantly added to their knowledge of
herbs and other medicinal agents. This profession has at-

tracted some of the most brilliant mentalities, and has made tremendous strides in almost all fields of research. With improved diagnostic and laboratory techniques, it has advanced upon all fronts so that today medical science stands in a position that commands the respect of all thinking people.

It is a far cry from the ignorant witch doctor to the modern, well-trained physician with his knowledge of herbs, synthetic drugs, glandular substances, vitamins, and minerals, to mention only one side of his knowledge. No matter how strongly one may feel regarding the efficacy of mental and spiritual treatment—and I am convinced it is the highest form of therapeutics—only the ignorant or mentally lopsided would refuse the recognition due to the science of medicine for its many achievements.

Within this field of material practice, however, many changes have taken place.

Allopathy: As medicine became an organized body of knowledge, its members were agreed that large doses of drugs were necessary. Thus the first school of medicine was the allopathic, which dosed our grandfathers with liberal quantities of herbs and herbal extracts and sometimes with some rather queer mixtures of other things not quite so nice.

Homeopathy: But in 1796, a German physician named Samuel Hahnemann startled the medical world with the pronouncement that current medical practice was all wrong. He argued that infinitesimal doses of drugs would produce better healing results than the large doses of the allopath. His homeopathic system was built upon the Latin phrase "Similia similibus curantur," meaning "Likes are cured by likes." He argued that a drug that would produce violent symptoms if given in an overdose would, if given in very tiny doses, cure a disease that showed similar symptoms even though the symptoms had not come from an overdose of drugs.

Immediately the medical profession proceeded to put him in his place. He was persecuted and hounded from pillar to post. The allopathic school contended that he was ridiculous and futile. They pointed to their many cures of sick people as evidence that they held the true secret of healing.

On the other hand, Hahnemann argued that his theory was the true answer to disease and referred to a long array of cured people to prove his contention.

Please remember that these illustrious gentlemen lived in a day so dark that they did not as yet know even of the existence of bacteria. Consequently, they did not see what is the actual truth: that beneath both systems is the fundamental Healing Principle that is contacted whenever anyone gets anyone else well.

Osteopathy: Time marches on! In 1874, Andrew Still, M.D., of Missouri, asserted that both allopath and homeopath were mistaken as to the causes of disease and the true method of cure. Dr. Still argued in part that sickness is due to a sluggishness of the vital bodily functions. He practiced a method of bodily manipulation that he said would stimulate the circulation of the blood and the lymph, and insisted that the body needs no drugs. Many people were cured as a result of Still's treatment.

The allopathic physicians, aided and abetted by the homeopaths, who by this time had gained recognition and respectability, pounced upon Still and his osteopaths and proceeded to have them thrown into jail.

Now there were three schools of healing, each claiming to have the only true method and each either openly or secretly belittling the other. Then came the fourth.

Chiropractic: In 1895, a gentleman in Davenport, Iowa, named D. D. Palmer, advanced the theory that all disease is due to the impingement of the nerves as they pass out through the little openings between the spinal vertebrae, this pinching resulting in the diminution of the nerve supply to the parts affected. Thus the school of chiropractic came into being.

By this time, the osteopaths had gained recognition; so they joined their medical brethren in persecuting the newcomer. But the early chiropractors were zealots as well as practitioners; prison sentences only fanned the flame of their enthusiasm, and they eventually gained recognition in most of the States because their methods of treatment also got people well.

THE DEEP-LYING PRINCIPLE BENEATH THE
SPECIFIC SYSTEM

It does seem strange that these four schools, using techniques so different from one another, each insisting that it alone had the only true method of healing, should all get excellent results from their diverse systems of treatment. It must be evident to the most prejudiced person that there must be something that underlies all these methods, and that is the real cause of the patient's recovery. We must go beyond the specific system to find the real cause of healing.

Whatever this Healing Principle is, it must be the *only* Healing Agency, and it must be far bigger than any system.

It is our belief that none of these systems has pre-empted the field of successful treatment. The evidence that each one of them assists the sick to health seems to indicate that there must be a deep-lying Principle of Healing beneath all of them.

This Principle is not the exclusive property of any of them, but each of them must somehow reach down into it and tap it at some point in its treatment, as oil wells sunk by different and adjoining companies tap a common oil pool. A company may use steel derricks or wooden. It may have different drilling techniques; it may drill straight down or slant its drill. The important thing is, does its method get it down to the oil pool? If it does, it is successful drilling.

Infinite Intelligence—the Mind of God: What is this fundamental Principle of Healing? It is the Infinite Intelligence, the Mind of God, which saturates every particle of matter in the universe.

We need neither be superstitious in our attitude toward Infinite Mind, nor adopt a sanctimonious demeanor at the mention of the Mind of God. That Mind is the Intelligence that holds together the atoms in a rock by cohesion; that causes chemical elements to be attracted to, or repelled from, one another by chemical affinity; that causes the sap to flow upward in the tree; and that causes a leaf to turn toward the sunlight.

It is not a religious idea necessarily; it is a natural action of this all-pervading Intelligence. It is not something to be approached with awe and genuflections, but something to be searched for in everything that exists. The scientist in the laboratory, smashing the atom or peering through the microscope in an effort to find the origin of life, is actually studying the handiwork of God, and is seeking to follow the workings of Infinite Mind.

As man follows accurately, he advances; where he misinterprets, he is retarded.

Man, looking into the face of Nature, is looking into the face of God. He may not know it; he may ignore it or deny it, but the fact remains that the universe can rightfully be called the Body of God.

Too long have theologians beclouded the issue by surrounding the Deity with clouds, seraphim, and angels—a majestic, awesome Being whose wrath was a thing to avoid; in short, an extension of themselves but having almighty Power that He was ready to unleash at a moment's notice to punish the temerity of man.

The truth is that God is impersonal Mind just as truly as He is personal Spirit, and His activity as Mind is a matter of fixed, undeviating law. The earthquake and the lightning are not "punishments for sin," but are the movement of matter through the activity of natural law. The selfsame Intelligence that causes the earthquake heals the body. This may sound like a sensational statement. It is not. We shall know how to heal ourselves and others when we understand the working of Universal Law.

The physician, using material methods, will be a better healer when he finds out just what it is in his treatment that actually and finally produces the healing, for it is something deeper and more fundamental than his drugs or his manipulations that is the secret of the restoration to health.

HEALINGS THROUGHOUT HISTORY WITHOUT MATERIAL MEANS

This is proved by the healings that have occurred throughout history without the intervention of any material means.

The early Bible records show us that the people of Israel were healed of their serpent bites by gazing upon the brazen serpent in the wilderness—a kind of spiritual homeopathy, in which likes were cured by likes, if I might dare to suggest it. Mental and spiritual healing may or may not involve the use of material objects, but it is not dependent upon them.

Profane history records many instances of mental and spiritual healing before the time of Moses. The Old Testament is replete with mental and spiritual healings. Elisha, Elijah, Daniel, and many of the old prophets were spiritual healers, taking it in their stride as a matter of course.

All reached far down into an interior section of man's make-up and released that inward Healing Principle that lies within us all.

The teaching and healing method of Jesus: Then came Jesus! The Carpenter of Galilee brought a new message of healing to the world.

—inner cause: He declared that all sickness is the result of disturbed inner mental states. He taught that when these

mental states are corrected, the physical illness state will
disappear.

In the practice of psychosomatic medicine, modern medical men are restating the thesis of Jesus in their own language and are endeavoring to correct the disturbed mental
states that are the fundamental cause of sickness. Jesus has
had to wait two thousand years for scientific vindication,
but it is here with a vengeance.

—*a corrected spiritual life the solution:* While it is true
that Jesus brought a message of inner spiritual life, it is
also true that the heart and the fundamental of his doctrine
have been overlooked in the maze of theological dogma.
He did not talk so much about an ultimate salvation beyond the grave; a corrected spiritual life is to be the solution to the problems of earth life. The major portion of
his work and teaching quite evidently was connected with
the material, physical well-being of man. He taught a high
spiritual standard of life, not as a means to gain heaven
after death, but as the key to life abundant here and now.

—*man's mind one with God-Mind:* Jesus taught that the
mind of man is one with the Mind of the Infinite Thinker
throughout the universe. He taught that man and the
Father are one; that apart from the Source, man can do
nothing; that all man's activities are merely the working
of this Cosmic Intelligence through him.

Man's liberation will come to the degree that he can
become aware of the activity of this God-Mind in him;
and since it works by law, he can learn to put himself in
line with that Law when all friction will cease.

We might liken it to the smooth, silent flow of the great
Mississippi River, pulled by the law of gravitation toward

the ocean, rising in a ripple only when a rock or some other obstruction hinders its movement.

Jesus taught that so long as man goes along with the Universal God-Mind, with which his mind is one, there cannot possibly be any sense of friction, frustration, or inharmony; that man's mental states can raise obstructions to the God-Mind; and that when they do this, he suffers.

—*man a son of God:* Jesus taught the true nature of man —not a worm of the dust, born in sin and condemned by a shocked and horrified God; not doomed to a life of misery in a world that is hostile to him, and sighing with relief when death frees him from his slavery and ushers him into eternal bliss. He taught that man is of the highest birth and destiny, in very truth a son of God.

He taught that man is the master of his circumstances, but that he has been hypnotized into believing he is a slave. He taught that the world is not a hostile place, but that it is man's servant; that sin and sickness have no right to have dominion over him, and that the ultimate sin is blindness to this fact; that as long as man believes that he lies fettered, he will suffer chains of his own making, but that his privilege is to stand up, throw off his shackles and step out into the glorious liberty of a son of God.

Jesus had a marvelously clear conception of man's rights as a son of God. He had shaken off the world's psychology and dared to claim his birthright of entire freedom. His thought plumbed the vast depths of truth, and cut through the shallow thinking of his time as it cuts through the twentieth-century poverty of thought. His clear vision and understanding, his inner awareness of the truth of man's oneness with God, surpassed that of any other thinker the world has ever seen. His inner conviction of the inexorable working of natural, mental, and spiritual law enabled him to line up with the God-Mind and produce results that even today are regarded as miracles by poor souls with stunted vision.

—*man's inner perfection:* Jesus taught that man is perfect at his inner core. If we can visualize man as being represented by three concentric circles, we can get an idea of Jesus' view of man.

He taught that man in the innermost circle, at the center of his being, is Spiritual Essence or Being. This center is as God is, never sick, suffering, nor limited in any way, always perfect in health and happiness, at perfect peace, entirely in harmony with the universe and everyone in it. This is the unchanging side of man. Nothing ever ruffles him here, and nothing can ever hurt him or defeat him any more than it could ruffle, hurt, or defeat God. It is this spiritual center from which all healing comes, and from which all mastery of life develops. It is his personal world of Causes.

The outer circle represents man's physical body and all his material possessions—his personal world of effects.

Man possesses the power of *choice*. He can stand in the intermediate circle and turn his thoughts outward to his outer circle or inward to his inner central circle.

If his mental states are allowed to dwell upon his outer circle, with its sickness, pain, poverty, and limitation, these experiences are perpetuated through the creative power of his thought. If, on the other hand, he uses his power of *choice* to dwell upon the peace, perfection, and entire harmony of his innermost being, these qualities will be manifested in his outer life because man's mind has creative power.

Every experience is first an idea held in mind. Everything that we ever enjoy was first an idea in mind, and everything that robs us of happiness was likewise first an idea. Mind is entirely neutral in its creative activity. It works ceaselessly, even while we sleep, creating into form that which we mentally accept as ideas.

Every business house was first only an idea in the mind of the founder. Every home that is built is first an idea in the mind of the owner. Every sickness is first an idea in the mind of the thinker. The loss of a job or of friends or of security is first of all an idea held in mind.

Man sometimes objects to such a statement, because he has not always been observant enough to be aware of the quality of his thought. A thought is sometimes only a momentary flash before it is stored away in the depths of the subjective mind. Once there, beneath the level of consciousness, it is no longer recognized by the person, who sometimes indignantly denies that he ever has thought of such a thing.

But it is continuously worked upon by the great Law of Mind, and continues to send up feeling states for which we sometimes are at a loss to account. We can set it down as truth that nothing ever manifests in the outer life unless it has been accepted and stored in the subjective, which is more than a mental storehouse; it is the factory working causes into effects according to a Law that never varies.

Man's power of *choice* enables him to think like an angel or a devil, a king or a slave. Whatever he *chooses,* mind will create and manifest.

—*turning to the inner perfection:* Jesus stressed the necessity for keeping the mind turned into the Spiritual Center, and insisted that if this is done, spiritual perfection will flow through the mentality out into the physical. Conversely, if one's mental states are occupied with the outer world of his changing physical states, he will continue to experience that which he contemplates.

There is a great truth here, and one that is too often overlooked. Whenever man's attention is diverted from the eternal, unsick, undefeated Spiritual Center, which is the image and likeness of God in man—whenever his mind turns from the awareness of this Spiritual Center, then and then only can physical manifestations of illness become apparent.

Jesus' method of healing consisted in denying the reality of the outward pathological appearance and affirming the reality of man's inner perfection.

This is the only method Jesus ever used. He placed no reliance upon concentration, will power, hypnotism, or any of our well-known psychological processes. He always called into action the higher Law of Spirit contemplating its own reflection as a perfect image, then the formative action of Mind producing that reflection of perfect image in the body, mind, and circumstances of the patient.

In that day, it was a beautiful philosophy; today it also has scientific proof. But even in that day, it was more than a theory; Jesus furnished pragmatic proofs in his numerous healings, which puzzled the leaders of his day, and have continued to puzzle some investigators until the present. Many concluded that he must have supernatural powers, in spite of the fact that he insisted that they too could heal the sick if they followed his mental and spiritual method.

Thus the world slept for twenty centuries, and has groaned under its burdens. If the message of Jesus had been correctly interpreted, the entire course of history would have been changed. Wars would never have been necessary. Sickness and poverty would have been eliminated entirely or reduced to a negligible amount, manifesting only through those of lowest spiritual understanding, and there would have been fewer and fewer of these darkened souls as time passed.

The astounding growth of scientific investigation regarding the nature of the universe is bringing a recurrence and validation of Jesus' teaching. The two are converging, and the point at which they come together is the field of healing. Every twenty-four hours, thousands of men and women are stepping across the boundary into the field of mental and spiritual treatment, following the true interpretation of the words of Jesus and other great healers and teachers.

METHOD OF SUCCESSFUL PRACTITIONERS TODAY

This is the method used today by successful mental and spiritual practitioners and consultants.

Treatment takes place wholly within mind of practitioner: A point that must be made clear is that the treatment takes place wholly within the mind of the practitioner. He does not try to influence the mind of the patient except as he may enter into an explanation of thought processes for the purpose of clarifying the patient's understanding.

When we come to the actual methods to be used in

giving a spiritual treatment, we shall see that the practitioner's whole effort during a treatment is to convince *himself* beyond the shadow of a doubt that this person for whom he is working is perfect as seen by the Infinite Thinker, and to remove from his own mind any belief in the idea of imperfection concerning his patient.

Since we see evidences of Cosmic Intelligence working away out among the stars, we believe that we are surrounded by an ocean of Mind that exists into infinity; that this Mind is the only Mind in the universe; and that when anyone thinks, he does so by using this Mind. What we call individual minds are in reality only single drops in this ocean of Mind; yet they are this One Mind. Mind is indivisible; therefore, what is known at one point in Mind can be known immediately at all points in Mind.

Spirit is ultimate Reality: The patient, complaining of sickness, contacts the practitioner. His distress is very real to him as the evidence comes to him through his senses. The practitioner knows that the evidence of the senses *appears* real, but is not ultimate Reality. That ultimate Reality is the unchanging perfection of Spirit.

Realizing that the patient has a distorted view of himself and his condition, the practitioner has to heal the false belief. He convinces *himself,* through argument and realization, of the falsity of the patient's notion. He positively must keep himself separated from the false belief that the patient labors under, as the rescuer must keep the drowning person's hands from clutching him. By convincing *himself* of the spiritual perfection of the patient, he sets in motion a *true* idea, which is opposite to the sufferer's false idea.

Both being in the One Mind, he then convinces *himself* that the patient knows that which he himself knows concerning this person's spiritual perfection, even though this knowledge at present may be entirely in the subconscious mind of the patient, and therefore not yet recognized. By holding steadily to his conviction of the spiritual and physical well-being of the patient in spite of all apparent evidence to the contrary, he becomes the rescuer who brings the drowning person back to shore. Eventually, the patient substitutes the perfect thought of the practitioner for his own imperfect thought, and the healing manifests itself.

The reader of this book can become his own practitioner by following the method of experienced practitioners.

Here is the way illness often develops: A person begins to experience physical distress. He recalls a friend who had similar symptoms and who became seriously ill or perhaps died. His fear begins to rise. Soon he is caught up in a highly emotional state. The picture becomes increasingly menacing and reflects itself in more painful, actual physical symptoms.

Now is the time for him to use the correct spiritual method of healing. He must immediately check the rising emotion and turn to his spiritual perfection, knowing that the thought is the inner reality and the symptoms are only the shadows thrown by that thought.

His changed mental picture now begins to assert itself and, held unwaveringly, it ultimately becomes form. His mind has healed him.

It might be asked here whether the practitioner does not use a subtle form of suggestion. To this we might answer that if the patient merely imagined he had the disorder, and the practitioner merely imagined he was made well, then the whole procedure would be a kind of unreal, dream experience. There must be some law by which physical results are induced in the patient by the practitioner.

THE LAW OF MIND BY WHICH
PHYSICAL RESULTS COME

This Law might be briefly stated as follows:

The mental image is the reality, and outer form is merely the projection of this reality. Since the mind is older than the body, it has created body. In fact, it is continuously re-creating the human body—a single cell at a time. Scientists now tell us that ninety-eight per cent of the body is completely replaced every year. The mind, however, remains continuous, recalling childhood experiences seventy, eighty, a hundred years later.

Mind, then, must be the cause, and body the effect. Mind must be the substance, and body the shadow. The shadow is always determined by the character of the substance; therefore, the bodily conditions that follow a treatment are of necessity a duplication of the mental conviction held first by the practitioner, and sooner or later accepted by the patient.

When the person is treating himself, both the awareness and the acceptance of perfection must, of course, be his.

Hundreds of well-authenticated cases bear out the statement that mind molds the body. History is full of instances in which physical marks were placed upon the body by continued mental contemplation of particular types of wounds. Certain devout Roman Catholics have practiced a religious exercise called "Contemplating the Wounds of Jesus." In hundreds of proved instances, these devotees have actually produced in their own flesh the marks of the wounds in hands, feet, side, or brow. In one notable case, that of St. Francis of Assisi, a worshiper of great devotion and consecration, scar tissue formed in the palms of his hands in the shape of nailheads so real that it is said that those preparing him for burial endeavored with pincers to draw the nails out of his hands.

If the Law of Mind will work against the tendency of nature by producing morbid tissue in the place of good flesh, how much more confidence should we have when we approach the matter of changing morbid tissue into healthy substance.

The person who understands the power and scope of the Law of Mind has at his disposal a source of energy that is infinite. His confidence, therefore, rests not upon any intellectual force that is his alone, not upon any supposed "gift of healing" granted to him as an individual or to anyone else as a "healer," but upon something far greater than any man, which is Cosmic Intelligence dedicated to his use and guided by his direction.

This is why we say that a treatment is *a definite movement of thought in a specific direction, to accomplish a specific result by reflecting itself in material form.*

This is not a gift, the peculiar possession of a favored few; it is given to everyone. The reader of this book has as much access to it as the greatest teacher has. It is his the moment he mentally accepts the truth that it is his, and proceeds to give to the Law the quality of thought that he wants to see brought into form.

No "big" or "little," "curable" or "incurable": This is why we assert that there are no big or little, serious or slight, curable or incurable diseases. We are dealing with a Power and an Intelligence that knows no big or little, because they handle a universe with ease. "Bigness" and "littleness" are relative terms. That which is big to finite intelligence is little to Infinite Intelligence.

The material physician, unaware of the Law of Healing, is limited to his own skill and the strength of the drug he administers. He must be accurate in his diagnosis, for this is the basis of his treatment. He must then wisely select the drug or the modality that fits that diagnosis.

He hesitates to reach beyond precedent although the daring pioneers who have gone beyond precedent have been responsible for the splendid achievements of medical and other sciences. He confines his experiments as far as possible to the laboratory, rarely making them public until a series of experiments carefully checked by laboratory techniques has convinced him that he has discovered a new material method with which to overcome the material condition.

On the contrary, we are trying to shake off the past, for it binds us by chains of doubt. "It never has been done" is the ball and chain that has hindered men from claiming their freedom. They said it to Columbus, and predicted he would sail off the edge of a flat earth.

We too sail out on an imperfectly charted ocean, daring to believe that we voyage to a new world in which the watchwords are, "We are the embodiment of what we think," "Whatever the mind can conceive, it can achieve," and as Swedenborg said, "The angels read man's autobiography in his structure."

Millions are migrating to that new world and finding it the land of freedom, peace, and health.

POINTS FOR SPECIAL CONSIDERATION

The reader who wants to become aware of the Universal Healing Principle and further to discover man's true nature, and use his understanding to his benefit will think through very carefully each of the fundamental ideas below.

A Healing Principle, operating independently of any medication by man, exists in the universe.

That Healing Principle is the Infinite Intelligence, the Mind of God, which saturates every particle of matter in the universe.

Man's mind is one with that of the Infinite Thinker.

Man's healing comes as he becomes aware of the activity of the Infinite Thinker within him, and puts himself in line with it.

Man has the power to *choose* to turn his thoughts outward to his experiences of limitation or inward to the unchanging perfection at the center of his being.

If man keeps his mind turned in to the Spiritual Center, its perfection will flow out into his body and affairs.

To Infinite Intelligence, there is no "big" or "little," "hard" or "easy," "curable" or "incurable."

CHAPTER IV

How to Build Strong Faith

The finest builder of faith that we shall ever see is right before our eyes.

Perhaps the greatest difficulty encountered by the person stepping over into the field of mental and spiritual healing is his feeling of lack of confidence. He says, "I believe this is the truth, and I see people who seem to have plenty of faith in it, but it seems as if I am naturally skeptical because I seem unable to work up a strong faith no matter how hard I try."

WHAT FAITH IS NOT AND WHAT IT RESTS ON

These people are getting the cart before the horse. Faith is not an emotional state that one "works up." It is not something like air that we pump into a tire and carry around. Faith does not lie in the feeling that we develop.

Faith always rests upon its object, and when that object is strong enough, there is no question of faith. Faith naturally follows knowledge. We first get the knowledge, and then we become aware that we already have the faith; that it came of its own accord when it found a substantial enough object upon which to rest.

I once drove an automobile across frozen Lake Geneva, in Wisconsin, not because I was naturally courageous, but because I had been assured that the ice was several feet thick, and I saw men sawing blocks of ice and noted the thickness. Instead of standing by and saying, "I wish I could work up enough faith or courage to drive on the lake," I found my faith was there the moment I knew how solidly the lake was frozen.

A traveler in a strange country would find it hard to work up a faith that a new-found fruit was not poisonous. But seeing others eat it without harm, he would not have to whip up his faith, for he would have faith immediately.

Any kind of faith is based upon observation and knowledge, and it is the purpose of this chapter to show how easy it is to have faith in the Law of Healing. If the reader will forget all about his faith or lack of faith, he will find as he goes along that his faith will be rising to the exact level of his knowledge of the Law.

Faith is not built upon uncertainty or upon revelation. We do not have to accept any sacred writings. The finest builder of faith that we shall ever see is right before our eyes.

MOST MARVELOUS MACHINE EVER BUILT

The human body is the greatest example of the working of Infinite Intelligence that the world has ever seen. Prop-

erly understood, its workings and activities will provide
the basis for a faith that will make anyone a healer of himself and others.

The human body is the most marvelous machine ever
built. It is greater than the Seven Wonders of the ancient
world, more complex than the most intricate machine ever
devised by man. It stands as a living tribute to the operation of Mind, for here, where we can watch it, is the clear-
cut evidence of Infinite Intelligence and the way it works.

A Plan, therefore a Planner: We can see a definite, fixed
Plan from the moment of conception until the last breath
is drawn. It is as though an engineer should sit down with
complete blueprints and construct, piece by piece, the several thousand parts of a machine, assemble them, and start
it running, with this added wonder, that this human machine is started running before it is completed, and builds
as it runs.

Watch the evidence of a Plan and therefore a Planner.

This body is the result of the union of a male and a fe-
male cell. This fertilized ovum, a tiny pin-point of Life, is
the beginning of the Plan. Wrapped up and hidden away
in this infinitesimal sphere of jelly are inherited characteristics of past generations. The color of the hair that is to
be, the eyes, the very tone of the voice, and the character-
istic inherited mental traits are all there.

We see a boy swagger or swing along the street, and we
say, "Look at that boy. He walks just like his grandfather,
holds his chin up in the same way." Yet the boy never saw
his grandfather, could not have imitated him. His own
father does not walk like Grandfather; so the boy's walk is
something that must have been hidden away in the genes,

those elusive carriers of inherited qualities in the original cell from which he developed, for once the cell is sealed it receives no more inheritance from the mother or the father.

In that infinitesimal first cell was the Plan—the Blueprint—that scientists have now discovered in the mysterious and remarkable substance DNA that is in every cell of the body. All the vast quantity of information needed for building these infinitely complex bodies of ours is coded into the long, slender threads of DNA, which are so thin they can be seen only under powerful magnification, but which if uncoiled would stretch out to five or six feet. Dr. George W. Beadle has estimated that if the coded information in that one cell were to be put into words, it would fill an encyclopedia of a thousand volumes.

That cell had potentialities because it was indwelt by the whole Intelligence of God, which immediately began to follow the Plan, the end of which it saw from the beginning. Resident in that cell was all the undivided Mind of God, whether one chooses to call it Cosmic Mind, Infinite Mind, Universal Subjective Mind—the adjective does not matter. For a period of two hundred eighty days, that Intelligence demonstrated its activity.

It had knowledge of structures that would be needed later, such as teeth, bones, ears, and laid them down long months before they would be needed. At definite intervening milestones along the way, certain formations began to take shape, always strictly upon schedule as though laid down by an invisible Architect.

The writer of the Psalms said, "I am fearfully and wonderfully made." Before the modern science of embryology, he would have been speechless, for the development of that mother cell into billions and trillions of daughter cells is romance, drama, and miracle all in one. Yet it is done so effortlessly and competently that it has become a commonplace to us.

At this point, it might be well to suggest to those who strive and strain to rid themselves of a common cold that Mind moved swiftly and surely to build a complete body with its systems all organized to harmonize with one another for the good of the whole. The completed Plan was laid out by Spirit; the creative servant, Mind, followed and carried out the Plan. Mind always lends its infinite creative power to the person who has a clear plan, for it knows nothing but to follow a plan since it is *Subjective* Mind.

The miraculous splinter: Watch Intelligence at work in the organism. That original cell divided into two by a process so complicated that it would amaze us were we able to observe it in its every change. Those two divided into four, four into eight, eight into sixteen, and so on until billions of cells were in existence.

And remember, these all grew out of the original cell. It is as though a carpenter were to take a miraculous splinter and construct an entire house out of it, getting floors, walls, sides, and ceilings out of it as he needed them.

The original cell was soft and jellylike; yet the succeeding cells were given different textures to meet the needs that Intelligence foresaw they would meet. Some remained soft and plastic. Some toughened into fibers, where they were bound together into muscles. Some developed into cartilage, thence into hard, unyielding bone.

Hinges and joints were all built in at the right places. Muscles were attached to the bony framework at exactly the right spots so they could move this rigid frame rapidly and smoothly over the earth.

Some cells developed into highly sensitive threads along which could fly the lightninglike messages sent by the resident of this growing temple, Mind. Short cuts were built into this nervous system so that some pain impulses would not have to take the time to reach up to the brain and back to the point of pain. Ordinarily the sensory nerves carry the message of pain to the brain, and the message is sent back along the motor nerves to move the hand away. But in certain dangerous contacts—for example, a finger touching a red-hot stove—the pain message rushes up a sensory nerve to a junction point and back down a motor nerve to the finger, causing a withdrawal of the finger before the brain realizes what is going on.

And all this is built before the child is completed.

By and by, certain specially endowed cells formed into tiny clusters, the endocrine glands, through which Mind would throw together materials taken from the food, forming hormones which would govern a multitude of activities, including the processes of life and death.

Some cells were built into a tiny powerful pump, the heart, the most durable organ in the body, which many people worry about far too much, for it will continue to do its work valiantly even when it has had very hard treatment. Some cells were formed into pipes and tubes of various sizes, arteries having three walls while capillaries have only one. Intelligence builds the proper walls for the proper work.

As the bones developed, openings were left in them at exact spots, little round or odd-shaped holes through which nerves and blood vessels should pass to various parts of the body. Similarly, openings were left in ligaments and muscles. The inguinal ring, in the groin, is an opening left in a muscle for nerves and blood vessels to pass from the abdominal section down into the legs. Hernia sometimes occurs at this spot.

Consider the marvelous intelligence at work in the building of the eye. No scientist knows just how it is done, but Mind knows the formula for thinning the skin over the forming retina, and gradually making it translucent so we can see through it. It constructs the eye in separate sections, each of which is distinct in structure, yet all of them together working as a harmonious unit when brought together in the organ of vision.

It creates the crystalline lens, making it wonderfully elastic so it can contract or flatten out to take in near or far objects of vision. It constructs two chambers containing fluids. It builds the optic nerve with its myriad nerve-endings pointed outward so they can catch certain vibrations from the outer world, translating them in the brain into visioned objects.

Another remarkable thing about the eye is its provision for adequate protection. All of us have noticed that one instantly blinks in the presence of danger to the eyeball. The most sensitive and the most easily pierced portion of the eyeball is the pupil. To protect the pupil, Mind has constructed in the eyelid a small disk of cartilage, very tough. When the eyelid blinks, this disk is brought over the pupil and acts as a protector.

Thus, Intelligence furnishes proper protection for the functioning of an organ that it has constructed.

The ear furnishes another illustration of the intelligent coordination of parts to form a perfect working structure. The external ear is the shell-like portion commonly called the ear. There is also the middle ear, which houses the drum and also three little ossicles, or bones, each separate but contacting the other, and called the anvil, the hammer, and the stirrup from their peculiar shapes.

The auditory nerve, which leads into the brain, is the counterpart of the optic nerve, which leads from eye to brain, and is connected with the drum of the ear. Sound waves strike this vibrable drum, or diaphragm, and cause it to vibrate at their own particular wave length. These vibrations are caught up and carried into the brain by the auditory nerve, which registers them according to their wave length. Thus we are able to distinguish a high pitch from a low, a sharp sound from a dull.

Wrapped away in the inner ear is a little bony structure called the cochlea, curled up like a periwinkle. If this were opened out, it would be seen to have the shape and appearance of a harp, the bony part being the base and back of the harp. Extending from this bony part are thousands of tiny little hairlike projections corresponding to the strings of the harp and graduated in length like harpstrings, which capture and record the pitch of the sound vibrations.

Thus does Mind build separate structures which, when brought together, co-operate to form a single unit, the organ of hearing.

Persons with poor eyesight or hearing should remember that Intelligence built those organs to function properly. It can restore eyesight and hearing, and will if it receives proper co-operation.

The timetable: As we see this structure, the body, taking form, with perfect timing as the various parts are brought together, it is as though a railroad were being built from the east coast and another from the northern boundary, timed and executed so precisely as to intersect at the exact moment.

In two hundred eighty days, Mind has built a complicated organism of belts, pulleys, hinges, trap doors, with kitchen, pantry, dining room, complete hot-water system, air conditioned to keep the temperature at 98.6 degrees, and even wired for sound.

REBUILDING, REPAIR; DEFENSE, PROTECTION

It is not reasonable to suppose that Mind then loses all interest in the complicated organism it has built. It dwells within it and uses it as a vehicle for its activities. We do not have to plead with it to heal; it actually wants a fit vehicle.

This Intelligence whose work we watch in the body is the same Mind that knows perfectly how to heal the structure it has built. It knew how to build those cells out of nothing; it certainly knows how to build new cells when something has happened to sicken the old ones. Our part is to co-operate with it in the quality of our thought.

The need for man's co-operation: We must always remember that this thought activity, while highly intelligent, able to build any structure perfectly, is nonreasoning Intelligence. It knows the mechanics of building cells, but it must always follow a plan. It will follow a disease pattern as quickly as it will follow a health pattern.

Thus the person whose thought-life is characterized by destructive thought—with its fears, hates, grudges, envies, with its discussion of, and absorption in, sickness and sadness—is creating a thought-pattern that the ceaseless activity of Mind fabricates into illness forms—quite impersonally but none the less certainly.

Our privilege is to take definite steps to change that underlying thought-pattern into one of health, love, peace, happiness. This done, Mind follows that pattern, and the resultant happiness and health are not a miracle, but the plain working of Universal Law.

Following out our statement of the nonreasoning working of Subjective Mind, we note that while it knows exactly how to build, it does not reason as to whether it is right or wrong to build certain cells in a certain place.

Alexis Carrel, M.D., in *Man the Unknown* refers to the fact that this Intelligence will arrange cells even where they are not needed. In the laboratory, when he took a group of epithelial cells, which are those protecting the surface of the skin, and scattered them around in a suitable medium, they soon arranged themselves in a pavement mosaic, just as they would do in the skin, to protect a raw surface that was not there.

It seems that it is their nature to arrange themselves in this way because Spirit has designed epithelial cells for the purpose of protecting surfaces. Mind, therefore, obediently working according to the Plan, always seeks to build them into this mosaic wherever they are.

Mind knows the mechanics of joining cells together. A surgeon could graft a flap of skin onto the tip of a person's nose, and this nonreasoning Intelligence would grow it there to flap in the breeze even though it is not needed.

It is for this reason that Mind can destroy the body as well as build it. Thus it receives our morbid thought and follows it faithfully to produce pathological conditions. In other words, Mind ceaselessly builds new cells, but the quality of those cells is determined by the quality of our thought, for thought is the pattern.

Nevertheless, many people are stricken with disease and healed without ever knowing anything about it, because Mind moves swiftly and effortlessly into activity to provide for the defense and the repair of the body.

A calcium wall: For example, large numbers of people develop tuberculosis at some period of their lifetime, but never know they have it or have had it. The person in whom a stubborn chest cold lingers for as much as two months may have incipient tuberculosis. The lung may have been invaded by the tubercle bacillus, which has found a settling place and is commencing to multiply. If one has not sufficient calcium, phosphorus, and other repair material in his blood, his case will probably go on into active tuberculosis. If he has sufficient minerals and vitamin D, Mind calls upon the repair forces of the body to rush up their reserves to the invaded lung area.

These repair crews immediately proceed to build a calcium wall around the affected spot, shutting it tightly off from the remainder of the lung and sealing the bacilli within what virtually amounts to a prison of lime. Postmortem dissections very frequently reveal these tubercular scars in persons who lived to a ripe old age, never dreaming that they had once suffered from tuberculosis.

This Principle of Healing that operates when we are not conscious of it becomes a strong weapon in the hands of the person who gets his eyes open to it, and learns how to co-operate with it.

A protecting apron: Suppose we note the way Mind protects the body in a case of appendicitis. We all have a serous membrane called the omentum, or great apron, suspended in the abdominal cavity. It is similar in size and shape to the tiny aprons worn by waitresses in tea rooms.

When the appendix becomes badly inflamed and ready to burst, it is not infrequent for this apron to surround the appendix and pucker itself into a tightly sealed sac that encloses the appendix. Thus, if the appendix should receive violent treatment or should rupture, the pus would not escape into the abdominal cavity to cause peritonitis.

Every surgeon who has practiced ten years or more has come upon one or more cases of this type, and when he does he leaves it alone with a prayer of thankfulness because he knows that that poisonous material in the sac will in due time be absorbed and neutralized by nature.

An entrapping mesh: Another example of the intelligent working of Universal Mind is seen in a cut finger. It is a little thing to us, and we do not fear it because we know that soon the bleeding will stop. But do we realize that this is a direct operation of Mind entirely beyond man's power to duplicate? That cut would kill us if it were left to man's unaided skill to heal it. No man lives who knows how to grow one new cell to heal a wound.

In a surgical operation, the doctor may perform the mechanical task of removing an appendix. Then he sews the patient up—another mechanical task—and here his work ends. He does not have the slightest idea of what to do to make those cells once more unite to heal that incision. If it were left to man's skill, the patient would remain for life like a football, laced together but always having the incision open. Mind, and Mind alone, grows those cells together and promotes the healing.

But to return to the healing of the cut finger:

A certain substance is kept in a state of solution in the blood as long as the blood does not come in contact with the outer air. When a cut occurs, and the blood begins to flow out into contact with the air, this substance changes its form, forming tiny threads or sticks somewhat like fluffy hairs. These form into a mesh in the wound and trap the white blood cells. Gradually, they form into a clot. This goes on to make a scab which effectually seals the wound against the presence of air.

At the same time, other white blood cells are rushed along upon the bloodstream to the cut, some to engage in repair and rebuilding, and some to eat up any bacteria that might invade the wound. Nutritive material is drawn to the spot and new cells built to take the place of those destroyed by the cut.

The new cells are built up from the bottom of the wound under the protection of the scab. If one should pull the scab away before the entire rebuilding is completed, the cut will bleed again, and the whole process will be repeated —formation of clot, scab, and so on—so that the repair can be completed according to the Plan of Spirit, held before the Intelligence operating in the body.

Man boasts of his knowledge, and he has a right to. He has made great strides in his acquisition of knowledge of the body. But at best, he is far from knowing the answer to the problem of Life. He does not know how to build one new cell in that cut, but a greater Intelligence does it quickly.

When, therefore, man says this or that condition is incurable, he talks from his own limited knowledge. In mental-spiritual treatment, we have gone further, relying upon that great Cosmic Intelligence whose Law of Healing we are coming to understand.

Thus we see cases, given up as hopeless by the skilled physician, healed completely and permanently by this Intelligence when directed by the person who understands the Law by which it operates.

We say, therefore, that there are no incurable illnesses, but there are incurable people. Those who insist that "now the doctors have done everything; it is of no use trying anything else" are incurable people. Those who give mental acceptance to the truth that with God (Mind) all things are possible are curable people.

Cement to weld: In a striking manner, Mind performs a seeming miracle in the repair of a broken bone. All that man can do here is to perform certain mechanical actions. The physician's knowledge is invaluable in setting the broken ends of the bone in apposition, and supporting the bone by splint or cast, but this is where he must stop. He knows, and is very frank in admitting, that man has not as yet acquired the knowledge of repair necessary to grow the bone together. But see how Intelligence comes to the rescue.

When a bone is fractured by a blow, the bruising of tissue draws blood to the spot so that swelling takes place.

With this influx of blood, nutritive and repair material is carried rapidly to the seat of the injury. While this is happening, the torn muscle fibers begin to change into cartilage, which is the forerunner of bone. Mind thus gets ready to hurry up the process of building new bone cells from the materials on hand.

A kind of cement is poured out to weld the broken ends together after the doctor has set the ends in line. Then as the patient keeps the limb at rest, Intelligence builds brand-new material into position, and soon the limb is better than before.

If Infinite Intelligence can do this, it can do anything we want it to do. Besides, it does all this silently, easily, effortlessly, and without any fuss.

The Power flowing into a sick body can heal any condition. Man becomes panicky. Mind is always sure of itself. Mind knows how to repair anything that goes wrong in the body. It knows how to build any kind of cell; how to snatch a person from the edge of the grave, with the expenditure of no more effort than man would use to lift a straw—in fact, less than that, for Mind is never conscious of effort or strain.

All these varied activities that are called into play, all this Intelligence that knows exactly what to do and how to do it, have been used to build this universe, to maintain and regulate it, to keep life on it, to carry on repair from time immemorial; yet that Power and Intelligence have not diminished nor weakened nor been depleted by a fraction. They are all about us and within us at this moment, ready to flow silently into motion in our behalf as soon as we stop obstructing that flow by our own mental barricades.

Haste to replenish: See how Intelligence works where there are large wounds accompanied by serious loss of blood. As the total quantity of blood in the body diminishes following the injury, the pressure in the arteries automatically drops lower; therefore, the blood vessels constrict in size in an effort to maintain the normal blood pressure.

At the same time, the various tissues of the body yield up water which rapidly makes its way into the circulatory system, thus restoring the total volume of blood to normal. The transfer of water from the tissues to the blood makes the patient extremely thirsty. It is always noted that an injured person asks for water when there has been loss of blood. It is Mind seeking to reestablish normalcy in the body.

We must recognize also that there has been considerable loss of red blood cells. The water restores the volume but not the quality of the blood; therefore, the red bone marrow and other storage parts of the body begin to pour out supernormal numbers of red cells until the blood is again built up to its normal quality.

Thus by a series of swift, sure moves the Intelligence in the body goes into action to save the body as rapidly as possible. Once more do we see intelligent, competent action which is far beyond the skill and knowledge of the best trained minds. This is the Intelligence that we use in mental and spiritual healing.

It should fill us with wonder to see the workings of Infinite Intelligence thus building, rebuilding, and restoring the body in emergencies without any conscious direction upon our part. It seems as though Mind has a consuming passion to save the body and to keep it at its highest efficiency. Health is natural; sickness is unnatural. Sickness never is initiated from God's side—always from man's. Man provides the obstructions to healing while God-Mind is forever attempting to keep the body in, or restore it to, its position as a perfect temple in which Spirit dwells.

Ammunition to the defense: Another example of this might be used. We could take any of the infective diseases, but we shall take pneumonia as an illustration. First, there is bacterial invasion of the body. Sometimes these bacteria are already in the body, not to kill but because they like the climate. When the body becomes excessively exhausted, they take over.

As they become active in the body, messages are sent to general headquarters with the news. Intelligence immediately organizes the body for a fight. All the defensive forces of the body are called into action. They immediately begin to manufacture antibodies, the shrapnel and bullets with which to defend the body against the invader.

Nothing seems to happen for nine days; evidently it takes this length of time to get sufficient bullets ready so the enemy can be attacked with reasonable certainty of success. Intelligence gives the word, and the ammunition is brought into action. The battle is now on in earnest between the invading bacteria and the defending antibodies. This period in pneumonia is called the crisis—the point at which the tide of battle turns for either the better or the worse. If sufficient antibodies have been mustered, the bacteria are annihilated; if there is an insufficient supply, the battle is lost, and the patient passes on.

Forts of defensive power: Space forbids our going into the many aspects of the defensive operations of Intelligence in the body. It is sufficient to say that there is not one part of the body from tip to toe that is not equipped to defend itself against invasion. Hundreds of tiny lymph-nodes are scattered at short intervals; these are the forts that are concentrations of defensive power.

Mobile units of the militia: White blood cells are able to travel with extreme speed from one part of the body to another so as to concentrate themselves at any point where infection may have occurred. They eat up the bacteria rapidly, moving up toward them and surrounding large numbers at one time, quickly digesting them. They could be likened to mobile units of the militia, sensing the danger points and getting there quickly.

All are under the direction of Mind, and our minds are one with that Universal Mind. We, therefore, have within us the power to direct this marvelous Intelligence, which knows all there is to know in the universe, yet is subjective to our conscious direction. This is breath taking in its implications.

Perhaps the reader is coming to see that faith is not something that we somehow work up in our ignorance. Faith rests always upon knowledge. It is not difficult to allow our faith to rest upon an Intelligence that is so all inclusive.

Later, when we come to the technique used in aligning ourselves with this Intelligence, we shall understand how it is that puny man can guide the Power that runs the universe. It is a fact, stupendous as it seems. Mental and spiritual healing is the result, not of tiny man's efforts, but of the ability to direct Cosmic Intelligence just as a welder directs the oxyacetylene flame which burns its way through steel, through which unaided he could not force his way.

CHEMICAL AND DIGESTIVE MARVELS

An entire book could be written about the various chemical and digestive marvels of the body. We shall mention some briefly.

The splitters: Digestion would be impossible without enzymes, which split up the various foodstuffs so they can be utilized in the body. These mysterious invisible substances are momentarily being created by Intelligence, used, replaced, disappearing as they do their work, and re-created to do the next piece of work.

Fantastic factories: The endocrine glands manufacture the most complex chemical compounds, many of which the chemist, with his rows of vials of raw chemicals, cannot duplicate. Yet Mind creates them out of the groceries we put into the body daily. Each of these fantastic hormones affects the others when they come in contact with each other, and if one of these little factories should quit manufacturing its hormone, death would occur.

Most people are familiar with the malady called diabetes, which ensues when a few highly specialized clusters of cells in the pancreas seem to go on strike and refuse to manufacture insulin.

A little capsule sitting atop each kidney busily manufactures adrenalin, which keeps the heart beating and has a lot to do with breathing as the asthmatic knows only too well. These adrenal glands are no larger than one's fingernail; yet so important are the hormones they produce that if they should not work the person would waste away and pass on within a short time.

Thyroid and pituitary glands also manufacture extremely valuable substances that control the weight as well as the sanity of the person.

All these and many more are made by the Master Chemist of the universe out of everyday foodstuffs.

And all that skill is at our disposal in healing. There is no physical condition that Mind cannot correct. There are no incurable diseases. I was healed of diabetes through the action of this Mind, and have since had the great joy of seeing thousands of men and women step out of despair and gloom into peace and health as they have been brought to see that this Mind can do anything. Anything!

A drink of water and a pinch of salt: Mind does not need any made-to-order chemicals. A person takes a drink of water and a pinch of salt into his stomach. The water is composed of hydrogen and oxygen; the salt is sodium and chlorine. Mind separates the hydrogen from the water, and the chlorine from the salt, and recombines them as hydrochloric acid, which it uses as a digestive juice.

HARMONY THE KEYNOTE OF THE UNIVERSE

Intelligence built the body with the intention of having it always function perfectly. Sickness is man's interference with this intention. Intelligence always contemplates the body as being in a perfect state, and works tirelessly to obliterate anything that would threaten the harmonious life of the body, or indeed of any single cell in the body. Health is nothing but a harmonious interrelation of every part of the body. Sickness is merely the breaking of this harmony.

Harmony is the keynote of the universe. Everything in the universe throbs with a steady, harmonious rhythm. Any disturbance of this rhythm spells unhappiness.

Rhythm of the universe: From earliest times, man has observed the rhythm of the universe. He has noticed that the stars come nightly to the sky; that the sun appears every morning and pursues its quiet course toward the west in rhythmic sequence; that the moon shows her face with rhythmic regularity; that the birds mate and molt in season; that the earth becomes fruitful and gives crops with regularity; that the tides ebb and flow according to a preordained rhythm; that his heartbeat and his breathing partake of the same; that physical functions in men and women have a certain periodicity.

Furthermore, he has noticed that so long as these bodily phenomena maintain their rhythmic sequence it is well with him, and that whenever the rhythm is destroyed, discomfort or even tragedy appears.

Rhythm in the thought-life: In modern times, it has been discovered that the same is true of our thought-life. We have learned that love is rhythm, while hate is discord; generosity is rhythm, while selfishness is discord; trust is rhythm, jealousy is discord; hope is rhythm, despair is discord; faith is rhythm, fear is discord; honesty is rhythm, deceit is discord.

Thus, as long as man holds his mental states in tune with the rhythm of the universe, his well-being is assured. When he allows discord in his thought-life, that well-being is lost.

The reason for this is that we are dealing with a Universal Intelligence, whose laws we learn through observation. Since we have seen that harmony is the keynote of the universe, the person who wishes to have Intelligence co-operate with him must co-operate with Intelligence. Disordered mental states produce sickness because they break into, and run counter to, an eternally established Law of Universal Harmony.

There need be nothing "churchy" in our attitude toward Intelligence. As reasoning men and women, we merely recognize the fact of Universal Harmony, and see that when we break into that harmony, God is not going to change to suit us; we must change.

INFINITE KNOWLEDGE AND INFINITE WILLINGNESS

The secret of healing, then, lies in unification with Cosmic Intelligence. Enough has been said in this chapter to establish the fact that this Intelligence has infinite knowledge of the way to heal, and infinite willingness to produce the perfect form, so that we can rely implicitly upon the flow of eternal Wisdom into and through our bodies when we get out of its way and stop hindering it.

"God within us is mighty to heal."

POINTS FOR SPECIAL CONSIDERATION

The reader who wants to build a strong faith in the Intelligence that built his body and is ready to heal it, and who wants to co-operate with that Intelligence, will think through the following from every point of view, and will govern his thinking accordingly.

The human body is the greatest example of the working of
Infinite Intelligence that the world has ever seen.

Infinite Intelligence has built a body that is planned and intended to be a thing of joy.

Having built the body in the first place, Mind knows how to
repair anything that goes wrong with it.

The Healing Power is within us at this moment, ready to flow
silently into motion as soon as we stop obstructing that
flow by our own mental barricades.

The person who wishes to have Intelligence co-operate with
him must co-operate with Intelligence.

The Intelligence that built the body has infinite knowledge
of the way to heal, and infinite willingness to do so, so
that we can rely implicitly upon the flow of eternal Wisdom into and through our bodies when we get out of its
way and stop hindering it.

How to Give
a Mental-Spiritual Treatment

*The more we learn, the clearer our understanding grows,
and we advance in our ability to treat successfully.*

The technique of mental-spiritual treatment can be handled
in any one of several different ways. In the final analysis,
each person must work out his own form of words to be
used and possibly his own method.

This chapter gives the method that I have found to be
eminently successful for me as well as for many others to
whom I have taught it during the past fifty years. If anyone wishes to alter it as he develops, he has the right to
do so as long as he does not vary from the fundamental
steps through which he directs Universal Intelligence into
action.

In speaking of the practitioner, we should always remember that anyone who treats for himself, his family, or

friends is called a practitioner in this book. We do not confine the use of the term to professional practitioners.

WHAT A MENTAL-SPIRITUAL TREATMENT IS

A treatment is a mental activity. It is a definite movement of Mind in a specific direction and for a specific purpose.

There is no need for laying the hands upon a person for whom it is given. Thus we dissociate ourselves from all types of magnetic healing.

Moreover, we do not use hypnotism in any sense of the word. The psychiatrist uses hypnotism so that he can remove the barrier of the conscious mind and lay open the subconscious for the planting of his own suggestions. I have no criticism to offer, for psychiatry has been the means of removing complexes and obsessions, and the psychiatrist uses much more than hypnotism. I refer here to hypnotism in order to clarify our position in healing. We do not use hypnotism.

We do not use will power to enforce our ideas or pictures upon the lesser will power of the patient. That would be using personal force. We do not use personal force.

We do not use suggestion as such. Suggestion implies the repetition of certain forms of words. We do use words, but these are only for the purpose of conveying definite ideas, and it is the underlying idea that heals. We have no magic formula that can be repeated in time of stress and that thereby removes distress. All this comes under the head of suggestion. We do not try to influence the mind of the patient in any way. We do not "send a thought," nor do we "hold a thought" for another.

A mental and spiritual treatment is completed entirely in the mind of the practitioner. We start with the fundamental truth that the person for whom we are treating is a perfect idea in the Mind of God, and our whole procedure during a treatment is intended to remove from our own mind any idea or picture of imperfection or sickness in the patient, whether we are treating for ourself or someone else.

Having satisfied ourself that Mind has created a perfect vehicle through which Spirit wishes to express, and having seen the marvelous way in which Mind rushes in to repair the body when something goes wrong, we then try to align our own thinking with that of Universal Mind.

We therefore act within ourself to erase any belief in the physical distortion that has taken appearance in the person for whom we are working. The patient has accepted the belief that he is sick. The practitioner refuses to join with him in the belief. We know that the belief in its reality is keeping it alive in the patient; therefore, we must believe in the Reality of perfection if we are to neutralize the false belief of the sufferer.

We know that there are not many minds; that is, that each individual does not have a separate mind apart from the mind of his neighbor and apart from Universal Mind. We know that there is just One All-embracing Mind in the universe, and that what we call our individual minds are just that amount of Universal Mind that we are using when we think.

We know that it is impossible for that One Mind to be

both sick and well at the same time. We know that other persons are well in the same Mind in which the sufferer believes himself to be sick. A fountain cannot send forth at the same time both sweet water and bitter; therefore, either well people are not well, or sick people are not sick. Both cannot be speaking truth when describing their opposite physical states. And from what we have learned from the universe, we know that health is normal while sickness is abnormal.

Further, we know that the Law of Mind is a Law of Reflection. We know that Mind works ceaselessly. Back and forth moves the shuttle of Mind working the particles of matter into a physical pattern, and this pattern is the exact reproduction of the mental pattern held before it.

Since the sufferer is holding a pattern of sickness, the practitioner must hold a pattern of health; and by speaking our word with confidence in the obedience of Universal Subjective Mind, we are thereby able to direct this Giant Worker to follow our pattern rather than that of the patient.

If working for ourself, we recognize that while our senses tell us we have a sickness, our objective mind must consciously and deliberately tell ourself that the evidence of the senses is incorrect, and must declare our perfection.

Everyone knows that during great excitement, such as a fight or a rescue, those engaged do not feel the pain of blows that would be excruciating when the mind is accepting the evidence of the senses. So it is possible for one to hold his thought in such a direction that he is oblivious of pain, nausea, and other unpleasantness. Granted that in many persons it takes some great crisis to enable one to do this, the point is that it has been done and can be done.

THE SEVEN "R'S" OF MENTAL-SPIRITUAL TREATMENT

A treatment is one continuous activity, but, just as a golf swing seems to be one movement but is several fused into one, as we watch our thought processes we find we go through approximately seven steps.

Relaxation: The first thing for one to do in a treatment is to secure as complete relaxation as possible.

Assume a position that assures physical relaxation.

Relax the mind. One cannot treat well so long as he is under the influence of fear, worry, anger, anxiety. This mental relaxation can be induced by quietly contemplating the fact that we live in a universe that wishes us well; that Universal Mind seeks always to push the good toward us. We might find, as most people do, that we are quieted and relaxed by quietly reading a few pages of some good book that deals with this subject. Many people use the Ninety-first or the Twenty-third Psalm for this purpose. But whatever the method used to gain this mental relaxation, it is a prime essential for successful treatment.

Now, since we know that both we and the sufferer are in the One Mind, and since that which is known at one point in Mind must be known at all points, it follows that our calm detachment from the trouble that grips the patient must at the same time be the real state of the patient even though he does not recognize it.

Because of this, very often the sufferer begins to feel better immediately he comes into the presence of the practitioner, or sometimes even the moment he has sent off a letter asking for help.

In other instances, this relaxed calm is not immediately sensed by the one being treated for, but the one treating continues to know within himself that in the depths of the Subjective Mind there is always a calm, and that the disturbed mental state of the patient is merely a surface emotion. Eventually that which is known deep within himself by the practitioner will be known consciously by the patient.

It is best to treat for the person by his given name and surname. To make it more definite, it is good to add the address. This is for the purpose of making the treatment specific. Thus one could say, "I speak my word for Henry Jones, of 158 Fifth Street, Chicago, Illinois, for whom this treatment is being given," or "This treatment is for my son John, who is here in this room with me now."

Recognition: There should be recognition of the fact that we are not speaking into a void. Our thought goes somewhere; it does not die or fade out. We are surrounded by an ocean of Mind, the Creative Mind of the universe, which receives our thought embodied in our words, and which immediately sets to work to carry it out into material form because it works ceaselessly in this way upon all thought.

There must be recognition of the fact that this Mind has the ability to create anything, and is willing to create the health form as readily as the illness form, because it is the Servant of Spirit, and man is spirit.

There must be assurance of the absolute obedience of the Law of Mind to the word of spirit, and the assurance that it swings its whole power in the direction in which it is pointed by our word.

There must be recognition of the fact that this ocean of Mind extends throughout the universe; that it is still the One Creative Mind away out in space beyond the sun and stars, in Chicago, New York, California, Georgia, Finland, Australia, New Zealand; that it fills all space in the city in which we live; that it fills the room in which we are sitting; that it fills our own consciousness and is our own consciousness as well as that of the one for whom we are treating.

Since the One Mind is simultaneously everywhere, distance is no barrier to treatment. We can treat successfully for a person thousands of miles distant. I have given successful treatment for persons on the opposite side of the globe. The beginner need not hesitate to treat for anyone anywhere.

Relationship: There must be conscious unification with this One Mind. We must know that we ourself, the one treated for, and this Mind are all one in the Great Whole; that there can never be any separation between them.

This person being treated for has entertained the false notion that he is separated from God. He may not have put it in these exact words, nor have recognized that he was thinking it. But the fact remains that Spirit is not and never can be sick; therefore, the person who suffers sickness could only entertain that idea because of the belief that he is apart from God.

The one who sees and knows his essential oneness with Spirit knows that he can no more be sick than God could be sick; therefore, this appearance of illness must be a distorted thought-form having no basis in Reality and having no separate existence as an entity.

The Law of Oneness is the fundamental law of the universe. Anything that is unlike the One cannot be real; therefore, this thing that has made its ugly appearance has no law to support it. It cannot have any true basis for existence. No place was made in the body for it when Mind created that body.

It may be painful and terrifying, but it is a false terror, just as the painful experiences suffered during a nightmare are false, for they disappear when the sleeper awakes even though they seemed very real during sleep. It has no rights in the body. It is a usurper, holding its form only by bluffing the victim.

At this juncture, it might be well to point out that we do not devote much time and attention to the contemplation of the illness. The more we gaze upon it or discuss it, the more false reality with which we invest it. We pay only enough attention to it to know what it is we are to treat for; then we turn from its contemplation to the contemplation of the spiritual perfection of the patient, which we know to be the actual Reality.

At any time that we find ourself touched with a sense of horror or disgust at the appearance of the trouble, we should treat ourself to know that it is unreal, and that it is tiny and futile compared with the Mind of the universe.

Whenever we find ourself thinking of an illness as "big," "difficult," or "incurable," we should swing out in thought throughout the universe, and fill our consciousness with the evidence of the infinite greatness, scope, power, wisdom of the Creative Mind, before which this ugly form is as nothing. Thus we refuse to unify ourself with the illness-form, and unify ourself and the patient with the Creative Mind and its marvelous Healing Power.

As we know within ourself that this is true, that this one for whom we are treating is perfect, we arrive at the place where the treatment is going to become effective.

Reasoning: But sometimes, in order to arrive at this inner certainty, one has to dissolve his own doubts. These may keep rising in connection with the reported incurability of the trouble—the fact that the doctors have said there is no hope. They may come from the evident acute distress of the patient, which the practitioner may take on as his own mental state. They may come from the fact that the person says, "I have been to other practitioners, and they have been unable to help me."

Whatever the origin, these doubts must be swept away before the treatment can be successful. One may have to go through a process of reasoning in order to arrive at this point. He may have to argue with himself, which is sometimes one of the biggest parts of a good treatment. He may have to say over and over until he convinces himself:

"I don't care what the doctors say. Mind can grow a broken bone together, and they cannot. Mind can make hormones that they do not know how to make.

"Mind operates through an anesthetic to still pain, and it can operate now without material means to remove pain and to bring calm, peace, rest, and freedom from any distress. I know that pain is not real because Spirit cannot suffer pain, and this body is pure Spiritual Substance in every nerve cell and every body cell. Where Spirit dwells are always peace, calm, restfulness, assurance, perfection.

"Spirit is at this moment at that very spot where that ugly, false manifestation is trying to make itself real, and it fills every single tiny cell with its own Presence. Wherever that Presence is recognized, it heals all false forms, and I treat my false belief to know that Spirit is all there is, and this entire body from head to foot, from innermost atom to outermost skin, is the residence of nothing but Spirit!

"Whatever is in there causing this disturbance has no right there. It has not the slightest authority or power. It has no ability to produce pain or suffering. No poison can remain a poison in the presence of Spirit, for God made everything good, and according to the Law of Harmony nothing in one part of God's Body could wish to harm anything in any other part of that Body. Everything in the universe co-operates with everything else in the Infinite Plan.

"I therefore treat myself to see no hostility, but only beneficent, harmonious action within this body. God is, and He is filling this temple with the Presence of His Peace, Health, and Perfection right now."

Realization: Once we have arrived at the point where we realize the inner eternal perfection of the one being treated for, we shall know it, because we shall have arrived at a place of quiet, calm inner assurance, just as though we had come in through a rough sea across a turbulent harbor bar into the quiet of the harbor waters.

This arrival at the inner realization may take one second or an hour. It will vary at different times in the same week because, after all, the one treating is still a human being, sometimes wrongly influenced by his own moods. By moods, we mean that as a child of the race he is subject to race suggestion. He has inherited a great body of race thought from a race that has known much defeat, sorrow, and sickness.

But we need not be bound by the chains of race belief, and the higher our knowledge of Law rises, the more we clear our spiritual vision of the clouds of negative thought, the more directly and swiftly do we arrive at this high point of realization—the realization of the spiritual perfection of the one for whom we are giving the treatment. If the treatment is for ourself, it will be the realization of our own spiritual perfection.

When we reach this point, we are ready to release our part of the work to Mind.

Release: We must remember to free ourselves from any sense of responsibility for the outcome of the treatment. "The Father in me, He it is that doeth the work. Of myself, I can do nothing," should be etched upon the heart of every worker in this field. We are never responsible for the healing, and no credit should be sought when it is accomplished. On the other hand, when we realize that we are not responsible for the healing, but are responsible for one thing, that of giving the Law the perfect thought-pattern, we are freed from nervousness and anxiety.

We now come to the place where our part of the treatment is practically finished. Up to this stage, our responsibility has been that of building the clear picture of the ever present perfection of ourselves and the one being treated for, of removing all doubts as to that perfection and all fear as to the ability of Mind to manifest health in this one.

Now we turn our completed picture of Perfection over to the Great Physician, Universal Mind, which we might picture as the Servant who has been standing at our elbow while we write the letter of instructions.

In effect we say, "Here are my instructions. You are a perfect Servant. I know that you will carry them out to the letter because you have never failed yet."

With this, we turn away and go about our other business, knowing deep within ourselves that we have given the Law the perfect thought-pattern, and that immediately it has moved into creative action to fabricate our thought into form.

In fact, we could use the exact words above as the method of turning the treatment over to Mind, releasing our word and our perfect idea to the only creative energy in the world. It should be a complete release.

If one finds himself returning over and over again to the person and treating too frequently, it is evidence that he has not completely released his word to Mind. If this is so, it shows that the practitioner is not entirely clear as to who actually does the work. His mental effort does not help the Law, which has all the power needed to complete any healing no matter how serious it appears to man. His effort is to one end, and one only: to present to Mind the perfect thought-pattern.

Once this is released, it is the Father at work, and man's feeble pushes are not going to help. So, if one finds himself giving a little push, he should check himself and say: "Well, I'm glad the Law of Mind is working on that. I know it is doing good, competent, complete work."

A simple illustration might help:

Let us suppose a battleship has drifted onto the beach at low tide. It cannot get off. What are we going to do? Hire a hundred thousand men to push it off? To one ignorant of the laws of the universe, this might appear to be the best thing to do.

But one man might speak up and say, "Wait a few hours for the law of the tide." Slowly the incoming tide brings the mighty supporting power of the ocean around and under that weighty battleship, lifting it as easily as one would lift a pin, floating it so that the engines can drive it again out to sea. It would be rather ridiculous for one lone man to remain straining and tugging in the water, trying to help the tide lift the ship, or pushing on the stern to help it out to sea.

That is just what one does when he continues to lift after he has released the treatment to the Law of Mind. Let it go and trust Universal Law. It will not fail.

Rejoicing: I have found it to be a good thing to give thanks to the Servant as I release the person to it. The Law is entirely impersonal and is not affected by our thanks, but giving thanks and praising the Law does something to us. It helps confirm us in our belief that the entire thing is now in motion, under competent management, and that we have started something that nothing can stop. As a rule, we do not give thanks for something that we feel we shall not receive; so this thankfulness is an indication that we really believe that which we have spoken.

REPETITION OF MENTAL-SPIRITUAL TREATMENT

The matter of repetition of treatment is one that should

be considered. I have warned against overtreating. But the question arises, "Is one treatment all that is necessary?" In truth, one treatment should be all that a condition ever requires. As far as we know, it was usually not necessary for Jesus to give more than one treatment.

But few, if any, persons have the vision and the illumination of Jesus. He probably had the clearest vision of anyone who ever lived. He had such a complete oneness with the Infinite that when he spoke his word, it was as the voice of God. "I and the Father are one" was not the hollow repetition it sometimes is in the mouths of some of us. It was an unshakable conviction because he knew it beyond the shadow of a doubt.

We fall far below his lofty ideal, even the best among us; therefore, we often find it necessary to repeat treatments. His unswerving certainty of healing was communicated in Mind to most of those he treated except in Capernaum, where "he did not many mighty works because of their unbelief."

Our vision does not always break through the unbelief of those for whom we treat. We must remember that the treatment is not completed until it is received with full mental acceptance in the consciousness of the recipient; therefore, repeated treatment is often necessary because of his beclouded consciousness.

As a rule, two or three times daily is the most that one should treat for any one thing. If it keeps coming into mind between times, one can say quietly to himself, "I am glad the Law of Mind is working upon that," and dismiss it.

When one has to continue treatments until there has

been a full mental acceptance of them, each treatment should be given as a separate action. We should give it as though we had never given one for this person before. We should start right from the beginning, coming to the full realization of his perfection, and releasing it to Mind with the same complete abandonment.

When one keeps thinking he has to give several or a series of treatments, he must guard against the tendency to admit that perfection is not there. A series is necessary in many cases. Some of the clearest healings that I have seen have come out of a series given over a period of months. Very often it takes some time for the sufferer to come to the place where he is no longer interposing any obstruction to Mind.

So, if a series is necessary, one must be careful not to look at a person and think, "This is going to take a long time." If he does, he is denying his own word, which declares the immediate perfection of the person for whom the treatment is given.

The practitioner must always keep foremost in his mind that all men are now perfect; that they have never been anything less than perfect except in their own minds and the minds of their relatives, friends, doctors, and anyone with whom they may have discussed their feelings.

THE PRACTITIONER'S PART

The practitioner never heals the one for whom he treats. His part is to know the eternal perfection, declare it, deny the Reality and Truth of every appearance to the contrary, and expect confidently that the great Servant, Mind, will manifest the health that the practitioner knows exists at this very moment.

Since mind is the substance and the body the shadow, as we brought out in an earlier chapter, then this illness has no Reality; it is only the out-shadowing of the distorted thought-form; and in erasing that distortion and substituting the thought-form of a perfection that has never been lessened, the truth of being again shines forth. It had always been there, and can never be lost. It had only been temporarily overlaid by an imperfect picture. In healing, we give the Servant once more the clear picture that was held before it when it was building the body of the unborn child.

In concluding this chapter, I might offer a word of encouragement. Do not become discouraged if at first the healings are not too clear. While it is true that beginners often get the finest healings, it is also true that since successful work in this field is based upon exact knowledge and clear illumination, the more we learn, the clearer our understanding grows, and we advance in our ability to treat successfully.

POINTS FOR SPECIAL CONSIDERATION

The reader who wants to learn the technique of giving mental-spiritual treatment so it becomes automatic will think through the purpose of each of the Seven "R's" and will note the natural, logical order of the steps.

Relaxation

We relax physically as an aid to relaxing mentally.

We relax mentally by clearing the mind as far as pos-

sible of discordant thoughts and by reminding ourself that
we live in a universe that wishes us well.

Recognition

We recognize Infinite Mind, with all Wisdom to know
and all Power to do, which receives our thought and sets
to work to carry it into form.

Relationship

We and the person for whom we are giving the treatment—if it is for someone else—are one with Infinite Mind;
therefore, illness is a distorted thought-form.

Reasoning

If doubts come, we reason them away.

Realization

We *know* this is the truth about the person—oneself or
another.

Release

We release this truth to Infinite Mind, the only Agency
in the universe that can bring it into form.

Rejoicing

We rejoice because we believe that what we have spoken
is now being carried out.

CHAPTER VI

How Is Healing Made Possible?

This chapter will lay the foundation for a scientific, practical assurance, apart from superstition or even theological belief, of the presence of a creative healing process that man may utilize.

The discussion carried on in this book is for the purpose of trying to find an explanation of the phenomenon of healing that is based upon reason and scientific research, rather than upon dogma, theological belief, and wishful thinking. While we concede that the seers and religionists of the past have contributed much illuminating material to our knowledge of God and man, much of it has been of the nature of special revelations which may or may not have factual weight.

The person who thinks for himself does not want to be compelled to base his philosophy of life upon something that God is supposed to have told to someone else either ancient or modern. A substantial faith can be built only upon evidence that man's reason can weigh and judge.

If, therefore, we are to accept the assertion that mental and spiritual healing is a fact, we must search for fundamental reasons why it is possible; and these reasons should be such as can be arrived at by the man in the street without bringing in so-called divine revelations.

UNDERSTANDING THE COSMIC CREATIVE PROCESS

Since healing is in a sense a creative activity—the creation of disease-proof cells in place of those that were susceptible to sickness—the best place to start would be with the Cosmic Creative Activity because all creative work must follow the same scheme. What is it? How did the universe come into existence? Is there a Law by which this could have occurred?

We firmly believe that the answers to all these questions lie before our eyes, and that the answering of them will lead us to see plainly why man can expect a creative activity within himself that will lead him out of the bondage of sickness into the freedom of perfect health.

Following a thread from earth to heaven—Leaving our religious literature aside for the moment, we shall suppose that we are sitting upon this planet, looking about us at the might of ocean and mountains, wondering about the sun, moon, and stars, the mystery of life as seen in vegetable and animal, wondering what it is and how it all came into being.

Or, more romantically, we can imagine ourselves on one of the Apollo moon flights, deep in space more than two hundred thousand miles, viewing our planet as it appeared to Astronaut Lovell, "a grand oasis in the great vastness of space," or to Astronaut Borman, "the beautiful earth out there," "that good earth."

*—a formed universe—*The first thing we observe is that we live upon a planet that is composed of matter, which may be gaseous, liquid, or solid in form.

Matter has no mind of its own. It must always be acted upon by an outside force; therefore, it could not have come into being of itself. It could not have created itself.

In searching for the energy-force that brought it into being, we must, therefore, go outside of the material forms of energy, such as electricity and other forces, which arise out of matter.

*—Thought—*As we said earlier, there is only one form of energy known to man that does not have a material origin. This energy is thought, and since thought does not arise out of matter, but acts upon it instead, there must have been an Intelligence capable of thought before there was matter.

So we are led step by step to the realization that the physical universe could have come into existence only through the operation of thought.

*—Thinker—*If there is thought, there must be a thinker.

We choose to call this Cosmic Thinker "God." We could use any other name and still mean the same thing. We could call the Thinker by the impersonal pronoun "It." At this juncture, we are sometimes assailed by those of orthodox faiths who declare that in using the impersonal pronoun we have done away with God, and therefore are atheists.

If by "God" they refer to an old bewhiskered gentleman, in glorified human form, sitting in a definite place above

the sky called heaven, surrounded by angels and archangels
singing "Glory, glory, hallelujah," and having the Book of
Life in His hand, in which are duly entered the sins and
shortcomings of man against the awful Day of Judgment,
a being who is slow to anger, but whose anger once aroused
is almost unappeasable, who places burdens upon men in
order that they may come forth as pure gold, then we must
confess that we have removed such a God from our philosophy.

One could well write a book titled "God and His Maker,
Man," in which such an erroneous conception of God
could be proved to arise wholly from man's imagination.
We have by no means dismissed God from His universe,
but we make no bones of the matter when we say that this
anthropomorphic monster exists only in the imagination
of the type of theologian who insists that this is God. Most
enlightened ministers today, trained as they are in the sciences as well as in religion, have likewise dismissed this
horrendous, naive concept of God from their teachings.

The God that we understand through His universe,
then, is an impersonal Intelligence—impersonal, yet not a
blind Intelligence. It is an Intelligence that operates
through Law, that is not swayed by personal petitions sent
up by peoples on both sides so that He will give victory to
their armies or will give them a rainless day for their picnic,
or rain for their crops when there is danger of losing them.

Let there be no misunderstanding at this point. We believe it to be entirely possible to get the victory, the rain-
lessness, or the rain. But it is done through an understanding of the true nature of God and of the Law of Mind
through which God works. One can pray, wring his

hands, weep, and plead to high heaven for assistance from God, as millions have done in the past, but the heavens will be as brass in their unresponsiveness unless one makes use of scientific prayer, which is prayer based upon a clear understanding of the creative activity of God in His universe.

Even God cannot set aside the operation of Law which He did not institute or originate, but which is evidently part of His own nature. To violate the Law of the universe, God would have to destroy Himself. This He cannot do.

Parents have pleaded with God to save the life slipping away from a beloved child as though they were talking to a Father who had a Son, and therefore would not want to break their hearts by robbing them of their child. When their fervent prayer seemed to go unanswered, they have cursed God, lost their faith, even hated Him. That child might have been saved if the parents had had a true conception of the nature of God, and had prayed according to Law instead of pleading according to superstition.

We must understand also that man has considered such things as climate and wars to be unchangeable by mental action; consequently, there is a very small mental acceptance of his ability to accomplish such change. This is often subjectively hidden in the depths of our minds so that should we attempt to do it, the subjective drag would be all in the opposite direction.

Jesus was not bound by such fetters; he had struck out from all preconceptions. The center of his belief was, "With God all things are possible, and I and the Father are one." He proved his control of weather conditions because his conviction was so firm in his oneness with the Father that he could command the law that governed the wind and the waves. He did not plead; he spoke his word with authority, believing and accepting the fact that the law would obey him.

Following a thread from heaven back to earth: Having seen the reasonableness of our belief that there is a Thinker back of the universe, suppose we approach it from the other end. We have taken hold of a thread on earth, and followed it back until it has brought us to the Cause of the universe. Now suppose we follow another thread from heaven back to earth to learn what this Cause might be, and how it has brought the universe into existence.

*—Thinker—*There must have been a time, before any universe existed, when only God was. Man, unable to conceive of anything that never had a beginning, asks, "Who, then, made God?"

Science is now asserting that time and space do not exist, and that in reality there are no beginnings and endings, only change in form. It is difficult for finite minds to grasp the idea that God did not have to have a maker, that He is eternally present Life and Intelligence. We measure time by millions of years, and say that uncounted millions of ages ago God must have had a start. It is not necessary to say this, because the very nature of Intelligence is such that it is not a commodity, a material thing that had to have a maker.

The simplest answer is, "God always was," because He is not limited by either time or space. We limited mortals, bound by belief in time and space, had to have a beginning. Let us not fall into the error of some theologians— that of making God an enlarged image of ourselves.

As Troward has brought out, God was present, not from

the beginning, because there never was any beginning, but before there was anything formed. He was present as Pure Spirit, formless and boundless.

Since there was nothing unlike Spirit, there must have been a desire in the Thinker to create a Polar Opposite, something which, having form, would exist, or stand out from the formlessness of Spirit.

Evidently matter was present in a formless state as a part of the Being of God. Science tells us in the principle of the conservation of matter that matter is eternal and indestructible. It is never increased nor diminished in quantity, its total amount remaining constant. We know that its form changes. Particles are continually separating from one another to assume new and different forms, but there is an eternal quality to matter as matter. So evidently it is as eternal as Spirit, being present in and as Spirit from all time.

Modern science tells us that all solid substances, when separated and disintegrated down to their ultimate particles, resolve themselves into their most finely attenuated form, which is negative and positive charges of electricity. In other words, trace matter down to its ultimate source, and it is nothing but energy in vibration.

—*Thought*—Since matter, by its very nature, cannot move itself or change itself, there must be an Intelligence that operates upon it to bring it into form, change that form, mold it, and shape it.

That Intelligent Agent must be Mind, which we have been calling Cosmic, or Universal, Mind. That Mind, being highly intelligent, knows how to form the formless matter into anything at all, but it is under the direction of

Spirit, which sets the Pattern for it to follow. It is Universal Subjective Mind, subject to the Word of Spirit.

We have, therefore, a reasonable basis for conceiving of the Godhead as a Trinity consisting of Spirit the Thinker, Mind the Actor or Production Manager, and Matter the formless Body, the intangible Substance toward which modern science is so surely finding its way.

*—a formed universe—*How, then, was the creative activity carried forward?

Spirit, desiring a Body that would have form, conceived of itself as having a Body, the universe, and moved through the Law of Mind to bring into form that which was an idea, or concept, in itself.

As Troward points out, first the Intelligence, then the movement of that Intelligence as Law (the Law of Mind), then the result of that movement, which was the material, formed universe.

This is entirely reasonable. It does not involve any superstitious approach to the Deity, and it is supported by what science has already discovered although naturally science does not state it in the terms that we have used, nor in the extremely simple statement of the action of Cosmic Law. This book is not written for scientists, but for the plain man and woman seeking a workable philosophy based upon reasonably provable assumptions. It is enough to state that many scientists express their belief that the creation of the universe could quite possibly have come about in the way we have indicated.

Creation was not a once-and-for-all act. It is going on ceaselessly. Worlds are being born and passing on just as people, plants, and rocks. It would seem that this resistless river of Mind, under the direction of Spirit, sweeps silently on day and night, in a vast Cosmic Creative Activity, forever taking the Thought of the Thinker and condensing it down into form. It is something that goes on regardless of man, and was going on for uncounted ages before man came into being.

UNDERSTANDING MAN'S INDIVIDUAL
CREATIVE PROCESS

Now we come to the link between the Cosmic Creative Process and man's individual creative process.

Since all matter in the universe is primarily One, and all Mind is One, man's thinking process is a duplication of the thinking process of God.

A thinker—thought—body and affairs: We know that man's objective, conscious mind has authority over his subjective mind, which does not reason but accepts the thought of the conscious and proceeds to carry it out, just as the Universal Subjective Mind does not reason, but is the Servant of Spirit, and accepts the Thought of Spirit and proceeds to follow its Pattern and carry it out.

Man, therefore, is the offspring of God, and as such has the right to share in the creative activity, limited only by his ability to understand this relationship. If he could understand and accept the fact that he is a tiny triangle, having identically the same three sides that God the Great Triangle has—the deciding, the creating, and the resulting sides—he could change his personal world, as those people who have grasped this marvelous truth are now doing.

Man's thought has power only because it is the thought

of God. It has creative power because it is a part of the Creative Mind of the universe. Any idea that man has, to which he holds steadily and clearly, is acted upon by the creative activity and will come forth into manifestation.

Responsibility to choose: Man has the power of *choice*, the ability to select that which he wishes to pass into the mold of thought, and having selected it, it will jell in that mold and come forth exactly as he put it in. Each man may select his own type of desire, and Mind will bring it into form. The responsibility is his to select that which he believes is the good. One man may desire health; another may wish money; another, happiness, peace, fame. Each can have that which he selects.

It is as though a great river were seen by different men as a potential source of power. One builds a sawmill, one constructs an electric-power plant, and one a flour mill.

The Power that creates: The same water, backed by the might of the river, flows over turbines or water wheels and makes flour in one plant, lumber in another, and electricity in another. The river does not care which each man selects; its nature is to flow, and it does it impersonally, producing different effects according to the way the three men adjust themselves and their plants to the law of its flow.

Each of the men may be oblivious of the fact that the same river is operating likewise for the others hundreds of miles distant. He may think of his individual water race as the most important thing in his life since through it flows the water diverted from the river. But the water in his race derives its power only from its being a part of the great river with all its driving force.

So man's individual mind, tiny in itself, has creative

power because it is one with, and a part of, the great river
of Mind. If it were the insignificant trickle that it appears
to be when thought of as an individual thing of a single
person, it would have no more power than he, through his
will power, could put into it. But our thought is a part of
the great Creative Mind, and is taken up by that Mind.
Here is where it derives its power.

This is why we say that in real mental and spiritual healing we do not depend upon will power. The strongest will
power of the strongest person is nothing as compared to
the resistless flow of Infinite Mind.

This, then, is the Power with which we work when we
treat for ourselves or others, and the more clearly we grasp
this great truth, the more complete will be the degree of
perfection produced through our treatments.

Faith in the Power: Faith, then, is not such a difficult
thing to develop. Faith rests upon a solid, substantial
Power, Wisdom, Law, which flows into action in specific
directions as we build the suitable thought channels to
divert it, and which creates as it flows.

All that tremendous Wisdom and Power is flowing
through our bodies at this moment, but in too many people it is as unused as the power in the Zambezi River by
the people who lived along its banks centuries ago. Power
is never ours until we use it, but it is instantly ours when
we do.

Learn, and act accordingly: Every mental condition records itself in the body sometime, somewhere. The creative
activity of Mind, accepting the thought of man, works
steadily to reproduce that thought, whether it be for man's
weal or his woe. Disease is the result of some false idea that

has become too prominent. Health is the result of the contemplation of the truth about man when it becomes prominent enough. There is no idea of punishment or reward in this creative activity.

When we see this, it is our duty as reasonable persons to place ourselves in the position where the Creative Law becomes our friend, instead of remaining in the foolish position where it seems to work against us as our enemy.

We learn early in life that we must do this with all law. We soon learn that sharp things cut us until we learn to handle them with care; that eating green apples causes distress; that if we throw a stone through a window, the window breaks. The ocean is a menacing thing to us until we learn to place ourselves in line with its law by learning to swim.

Now, as man emerges into the place of the thinker, he is coming to see that his thought operates through Law. He is learning that every thought is photographed in Mind and reproduced.

As a thinker, therefore, he *decides* that he must do something about it. It is useless for him to sit down and complain about the way life is treating him, and about the fact that his body shows signs of falling apart. He must become aware that these things do not occur as a result of divine fiat, but are the logical outworking of his own thought, governed by Law. When he changes the underlying thought, the same Law will change the outward manifestation.

THE NATURE OF GOD

All this is done without any thought of influencing or changing the attitude of God toward us. It is not the old idea of the sinner in danger of harm who prayed God to save his life or his loved one, and who promised that if God did so, he would change his ways and serve Him all the days of his life. It is not the idea of the good we would do with money if God would only grant it to us.

Changeless: The fact is, we can never bargain with God. The Infinite Thinker is uninfluenced by our great need, our promises of repentance, or of the good we will do with the gift He gives. There is a certain Sphinx-likeness in the attitude of the Thinker toward the universe.

—*the gift is already made:* In Love, the Infinite has given all to man, and has provided a way by which he can take as much as he wants. That way is through law.

Man's business is to find out how law works, then practice his taking according to this method. When he does this, he discovers, sometimes to his great amazement, that his prayer is answered through his own co-operation with the givingness of God.

The gift is already made; it is man's to take. True prayer consists in getting out of God's way, and allowing the eternal good to flow into the life.

Thus we live in a universe of Love, which is also a universe of Law: Love, in the fact that all is already given to us; Law, in the way in which we become possessors of it. God is impersonal in the fact that He is not impressed with ignorant pleading; He is personal in that He becomes personalized through the gift as it becomes intelligently received.

We might illustrate this side of the Godhead in this way:

Let us assume that a certain wealthy man has decided to hold open house for the underprivileged children of his city. He has advertised widely that on Christmas Eve his house is theirs. They may come and go freely, enjoy the blazing logs in his fireplace, sit down at the great turkey dinner, and help themselves to as many gifts as they wish from the Christmas tree which servants keep loaded.

At the height of the festivities, one ragged little fellow is found peering in at the window, unable to believe that all this is for him. No one ever gave him anything for nothing before, and in spite of the fact that he sees other children just as ragged as himself enjoying the bounty of the host, somehow he cannot bring himself to believe that he could do the same. The onlooker urges him to go in and share the good things. But he turns away and goes mournfully through the snow to his poverty-stricken home.

The host, gladly seeing the children helping themselves, does not see the little fellow outside. The gift has been made. The invitation has been widely extended. The acceptance is now up to the children. There is no personal ruling out or ruling in of any particular child. There has been an impersonal, general invitation, which can become personal through personal acceptance.

This, we believe, is what was meant by the ancient seer Isaiah, out of whose lofty spiritual vision came the words:

Ho, every one who thirsts,
come to the waters;

and he who has no money,
    come, buy, and eat!
Come, buy wine and milk
    without money and
        without price.

Why do you spend your money for
    that which is not bread,
    and your labor for that which
        does not satisfy?
Hearken diligently to me, and eat
    what is good,
    and delight yourselves in fatness.

The world has yet to see the possibilities of the life that completely grasps the significance of the givingness of God. The very best among us is often found in the position of the boy outside the window. On the other hand, here and there throughout the ages, isolated individuals have dared to believe that the Creative Law of Mind is merely the Servant, hanging an abundance of treasures upon the tree, and resupplying them as rapidly as they are taken off.

Jesus was perhaps the greatest of these. His mental acceptance was extremely high. He believed implicitly that Spirit has made all good things available to man, and that man, in poverty and in bondage to a false idea of sickness, is a slave only because he will not reach out to take the good.

We are only at the beginning of a new awakening to this great truth. Those who step forward into this Law of Freedom make wonderful demonstrations of its availability. Yet they live in a world that still cries out in its sleep at the nightmare of sickness, and the mass belief of the majority crowds them in so that the invitational voice that bids them wake up and live is often drowned out by the cries of a world in chains.

As the years and the centuries pass, however, the voice of truth will be heard more clearly above the crowd, and the crowd, hearing it, will come step by step into a new knowledge of the fact that life is not made for slaves but for masters. Each man can be master of himself and of his circumstances.

So gradually man will grow in knowledge of himself and the universe in which he lives. Gradually will the mass belief lift itself above the false belief in the necessity for sin, sickness, and suffering, into the light of Truth.

Approachable: This truth will grow when it is divorced from all superstitious belief in the unapproachability of God. God is as approachable as electricity, which is easily approachable when we come to it through the law through which it operates.

We can well afford to forget the conception of God as a Potentate upon a throne, and see Him as the benevolent Author of everflowing good. This impersonal Intelligence streams through everything and becomes personal to every individual who accepts this Indwelling Intelligence that is the Light of Life. This is "the true Light, which lighteth every man that cometh into the world."

Present in everything: "All things were made by Him, and without Him was not anything made that was made."

God makes a thing by becoming that thing. This is the only way that God ever has made anything. The body of man is, therefore, a part of the Body of God.

MAN'S LIBERATION

Spirit can not be limited in any way, and man is Spirit incarnate. Any limitation under which man labors is merely a false belief in the reality of something that is actually unreal. His liberation comes when he understands this, and when he dares to claim his perfect emancipation from the dominance of his false belief.

Spirit desires no limitation for itself; therefore, it cannot desire any limitation for the individual. When one gets to the point where he sees that in seeking deliverance from sickness he is not asking a great favor of God, but is merely asserting what has always been part of an Infinite Plan for mankind, he will have more confidence in his ability to throw off the bondage of fear that holds so many of his fellows. The fear is often the sickness; the physical evidence is but the reflection of the fear.

Every sick person is sick in defiance of the purpose of Spirit. Every sick person has stepped out of the will of God in this regard. When one understands this, and decides to return into the will of God, the Law begins to co-operate with him for his recovery.

Our health is our own responsibility. No one else can give it to us, and no one else can take it away from us. We must make the change in mind. A practitioner can help us make that change, but the final responsibility is upon us.

The moment we have made that change and have reversed our previous attitude of struggling upstream against the flow of universal health, we begin to be carried along effortlessly upon those universal currents of health.

As we have repeatedly said, the effort in healing is not

ours. Ours is to make the *choice* and go along with the
stream. Then the consequent lack of resistance to universal
Law means that once more we are "in tune with the Infinite," and we come into the realization that Jesus was stating the simple truth when he averred, "The Father in me,
He it is that doeth the work."

Health is a simple matter, but we have made it complicated and difficult. Good health is the recognition that
man's body is a living Presence just as the universe is; that
it is not necessary to strain and struggle in order to enjoy
that health; and that the spiritual perfection is already
there awaiting our recognition.

A woman once said to me, "Since I was a little girl I have
had to use laxatives. Now at seventy I believe it is too late
to rectify the condition. Do you think it would be possible
to create perfection now?"

"Perfection is there now, and has always been there," I
replied, "but your parents taught you that it was not there,
and in the succeeding years you kept telling yourself that
it was not there. You can experience complete freedom
from laxatives for the remainder of your life if you will
allow that false belief in imperfection to be healed."

She did allow the false belief to be healed, and she did
experience complete freedom. A miracle? No! It is the normal functioning of a machine that was always intended to
function normally, but which for seventy years had been
hindered by a distorted belief.

Sickness is the greatest miracle in life, for it is the nega-
tion of Universal Law. Health is the most normal thing in
life. Anyone can have it who will stop telling himself that

he cannot have it, and who will approach it from the stand-point of Universal Law.

POINTS FOR SPECIAL CONSIDERATION

The reader who wants to understand why healing is possible and to increase his belief in the naturalness of good health will think through the following statements from every point of view.

Man, as the offspring of God, has the right to share in the creative activity.

Since all Mind is one, man's thinking process is a duplication of the thinking process of God.

Man's objective, conscious mind has authority over his sub-jective, subconscious mind, which does not reason but accepts the thought of the conscious mind and proceeds to carry it out just as in the Cosmic Creative Process.

Man's individual mind has creative power because it is one with, and a part of, the great river of Mind.

All that tremendous Wisdom and Power is flowing through our bodies at this moment.

When one gets to the point where he sees that in seeking de-liverance from sickness he is not asking a great favor of God, but is merely asserting what has always been part of an Infinite Plan for all mankind, he will have more con-fidence in his ability to throw off the bondage of fear that holds so many of his fellows.

CHAPTER

VII

Should We Refuse Medical Assistance?

We must face the fact that people vary in their spiritual perception and in their ability to receive healing, at the same time remembering that we are dealing with perfect Law, which can operate perfectly where the level of acceptance is high.

A question that has often puzzled the newcomer to spiritual healing is, "Must I give up entirely my reliance upon all material means of assistance?" It can be answered either yes or no.

VARYING LEVELS OF MENTAL ACCEPTANCE

We know that we are working with perfect Law, which knows how to heal any condition no matter how serious it may appear to be. But, on the other hand, all men do not have the same height or depth of consciousness, and this must be taken into consideration.

In saying this, we are not retreating from our stand that any condition can be healed solely through mental action.

It is difficult for some people, after a lifetime of reliance upon material means, to soar instantly to the heights of understanding. Spiritual vision is usually a matter of growth. It is less frequently a matter of instantaneous revelation.

The person who seems best to have understood the infallible working of spiritual Law seems also to have exercised a sane, reasonable attitude toward the sick. Jesus did not always use the same approach to healing although he always used the same Principle.

Jesus took people at the level upon which he found them. In some instances, he spoke the word, and they were healed. In others, he touched the sick. In at least one instance, he used material means when he anointed with clay the eyes of the blind man. He knew there was no particular healing virtue in clay of itself. But he knew that this man required the crutch of material action, and he did not hesitate to use it.

But Jesus knew that beneath it all the healing was accomplished through the operation of identically the same healing Principle that healed when he spoke his word.

Those who came to him varied greatly in their mental level of acceptance. Some were healed at a great distance, in neighboring countries. Some stood afar off and cried to him. Some pressed close to him. One poor woman felt that she would be healed if only she could touch the hem of his garment.

We must face the fact that people vary in their spiritual

perception and in their ability to receive healing, at the same time remembering that we are dealing with perfect Law, which can operate perfectly where the level of acceptance is high.

We cannot agree with those teachers who refuse to treat a person if he is consulting a doctor or using some form of material treatment. The practitioner should remember that he may have a high consciousness, while the one being treated for may have deep subjective fear-tendencies that he may not even have recognized, and that come together to impel him to rely in part upon material means.

Anything that helps the patient to be receptive to the idea of health is of assistance in treatment even though the practitioner knows that his own work is being done wholly in Mind, as Jesus recognized while treating the blind man.

ONE UNIVERSAL HEALING PRINCIPLE

If we grant the existence of a Universal Healing Principle in the universe, we must agree that whenever the material physician gets healing results, they must come from contacting that Principle, and not from any inherent healing power in the medium of medication.

If Jesus allowed the woman to touch his garment, and helped the dim faith of the man by using clay, it would seem reasonable for us to allow the person to contact the healing Principle through some material means if some such prop to his faith is needed.

Just as some physicians would rather see the patient remain in suffering than to see him healed through spiritual means, so, unfortunately, would some spiritual practitioners rather see the patient suffer than be helped through material means. The attitude of each is somewhat narrow and intolerant, and reveals an ignorance of the whole science of healing. Fortunately, these people are in the minority in both professions.

Since there is but one healing Principle in the universe, it follows that physical and spiritual healing must be opposite ends of the same thing. In the past, there has been a great deal of misunderstanding on both sides. Each should try to acquire a better understanding of the other's methods, because intolerance is always based on ignorance.

The two methods are by no means diametrically opposed. There can be no real hostility between them. They may appear to be separate and apart like two oil wells sunk into the earth on different leases; yet somewhere beyond our range of vision those wells penetrate the same oil pool.

The ever-unfolding knowledge of vitamins, minerals, and other dietary correctives can be a desirable thing, while other mechanical or drug methods can assist the healing by doing one of two things: they may remove mechanical defects and obstructions, and they may provide an object upon which faith may center so that the healing Principle may operate.

In this way, they draw the mind of the sufferer toward the expectation of recovery, because the physician's training and skill impress some people with the idea that he knows what to do to get them well, and when he applies his method, their thought turns upon it in the direction of health.

Now that we have said that, we can go back to our original thesis.

LAW OF MIND NOT DEPENDENT ON
MATERIAL ASSISTANCE

The great Law of Mind does not need any material assistance. There are millions of instances in which, without any material intervention at all, and solely through intelligent co-operation with the Law of Mind, people have been completely and permanently healed of such conditions as cancer, arthritis, paralysis, high blood pressure, heart trouble, anemia, ulcers, gallstones, nervous exhaustion, diabetes—indeed, every form of distortion from which man suffers.

PRACTITIONERS—AMATEUR AND PROFESSIONAL

The healing intermediary in every case was an ordinary man or woman who had attained a clear understanding of the inflexibility of spiritual Law. This person had gained the quiet inner assurance that the Law of Mind can be used for healing. Unquestionably, it can be used for healing by anyone who learns how to induce the flow of the universal energy called thought in the direction of healing.

People who are healing agents for themselves or others are not magicians. They are "plain folks" who have stopped resisting the universe, and have set their own thought-life in co-operation with it. They are not saints, nor are they tin gods upon pedestals. They are ordinary human beings, striving for happiness as all humans are, often all too conscious of their own shortcomings and sins.

Forgetting themselves, their weaknesses or strengths, they are gripped by an all-embracing confidence in the Intelli-

gence that built and sustains the body, and a firm conviction that Mind operates creatively through a Law that is
as certain as that of gravitation or electricity.

Two extremes to be avoided: Two extremes are to be
avoided: conceit and self-depreciation. Both are an evidence that the mind of the person is upon himself instead
of upon the great Creative Mind.

The moment a person begins to say, "I am a great
healer," instead of "This is a great Law of Mind," he indicates that he has forgotten where the power lies through
which he is enabled to heal. This person is now like an
electric flashlight shining by his own self-contained energy,
and growing dimmer as his individual battery runs down.

He ought to be like the electric light, with unbroken
connection clear back to the powerhouse, with a continuous flow of energy not of his own making, which never runs
down no matter how often it is drawn upon. One must
have faith in his ability to heal the other person or himself,
but that faith must always be reliance in Infinite Mind,
never in his own puny intellect.

At the other extreme is the person who constantly dis-
trusts and depreciates himself, who says, "I have a weak
will"—or little education, or no personality, or no flow of
words—"it is useless for me to think that I could help
others or myself."

Some of the most successful persons in the field of healing are inconspicuous, quiet, inarticulate people having no
academic degrees. But they have an unshakable confidence
in this great healing Law of Mind. Their minds are not
centered upon themselves, but range the universe, seeing
the hand of God lighting the stars, juggling with the

planets, pouring exhaustless life and vitality into all the living, growing forms throughout the world.

They have ceased to think of themselves as insignificant or uneducated. They have seen themselves as possessors of the Infinite Mind, one with all the Universal Mind that makes the earth throb and pulse with life. Just as there are no big or little problems or diseases, so there are no big or little people in Mind. All have access to the whole ocean of Intelligence. The only limitation is that which men and women place upon themselves.

Every person who reads this book has as much right to heal, and as open access to Infinite Mind, as the most famous person in the field of mental and spiritual healing. Law plays no favorites. All are favored.

Faith is not blind belief. Real faith involves two things: a clear, intelligent understanding of the underlying Principle of healing, plus a quiet inner assurance of the Power that heals.

As long as one's knowledge of, and confidence in, the Power are greater than his fear of the condition with which he is faced, he can bring healing. As long as his fear of the condition outweighs his assurance of the Power, he cannot.

These may appear to be simple statements, but they are set down in this almost repetitious form in order to establish them in the mind of the reader since they are fundamental to healing.

MENTAL AND SPIRITUAL HEALING DEFINED

At this point, it might be well to explain why the term "mental and spiritual healing" is used. Mental activity is the medium through which healings are brought about, but it is the Mind of Spirit that is thus active.

Three levels of energy: Energy may be applied upon three levels, each higher than the preceding one.

For example, physical energy transmitted through muscular effort can affect inert matter. We can pick up a stone and throw it, using physical energy.

The next higher form is mental energy, which is called thought. Mental energy dominates the physical since it operates upon a higher level. A fearsome thought can bring perspiration to the brow or blanch the skin. Shocking news can take away the appetite from a hungry man.

Spiritual energy is the highest form of energy and can impose its authority upon both the mental and the physical as we pointed out in an earlier chapter.

Thus one may work entirely upon the mental level, as the psychologist, the psychiatrist, the psychoanalyst, and the physician in psychosomatic medicine, and do good work. When, however, one proceeds to bring the spiritual concept into his thinking, his work is lifted up to the highest possible level of accomplishment.

It is noticeable that all those who have done the best work in this field throughout the ages have been those whose spiritual vision has been loftiest. We have stated before that Spirit works at the level of our mental concepts; therefore, that man or woman who is able to inject the highest concept of God into his consciousness will find that his treatments are correspondingly satisfying.

The best results are obtained when we recognize the marvelous intelligence of Mind, and rise one step higher into the recognition that this Master Builder, Mind, is under the direction of Spirit.

We conceive of Spirit as the only self-conscious Principle of the universe, Mind being not self conscious. "Spirit is First Cause, is self existent, and has all life within itself." It has the ability to will, select, and direct. Mind has the ability to obey, to be directed into specific activity, but it cannot will and select. The originating and initiatory act is always that of Spirit. It is then picked up and given form by Mind, which is the Universal Subjective.

Hence, we place full reliance upon the Infinite Intelligence of Mind and upon its ability to perform anything that has to be done, but we recognize that it is changeable in its action, creating constructively or destructively according to the *choice* made in our conscious thought.

On the other hand, we recognize the unchangeableness of Spirit, which is the Eternal I AM, forever dwelling in Perfection. Spirit, then, is the true norm by which we shape our thought. Spirit sees itself reflected in the universe, unchanged and unchanging.

Thus, when we say that imperfection has never really been in the body, we are rising to the viewpoint of Spirit and declaring that which is always seen by Spirit, namely, the eternal perfection of man. This, then, is the announcement we make to Mind, to manifest that perfection which Spirit always sees, and which, since we have cleared our consciousness of false images, we too can see.

When, therefore, we treat from the spiritual as well as the mental point of view, we see an eternal blotting out of the false picture, because that which Spirit sees is the only thing that can manifest. For this reason, spiritual healing is permanent, while mere mental healing might or might not be. That which is healed through spiritual treatment never returns; it cannot, because it is gone in the eternal contemplation of Spirit. "Their sins and their iniquities will I remember no more."

Spiritual thought-force has power over everything unlike itself. It has power over every apparent resistance. In the days of our ignorance, we thought of conditions as over-whelming, and we bowed in fear to them. But with the bringing in of the concept of Spirit, we now know that the truth that we announce is irresistibly superior to any con-dition. No ugly picture is big enough or horrible enough to offer resistance, because it is an unreal picture, and Spirit sees only perfection at the very spot where ignorance sees ugliness.

We must recognize that this pure Essence of Spirit is within us, erasing everything unlike itself, for it is "Not by might [man's physical force], nor by power [man's mental force], but by my Spirit, saith the Lord."

If the reader should imagine that we have been making a distinction without a difference, may we suggest that the results obtained by treating in this way will justify our argument.

We live in a spiritual universe. Dr. Bucke says, "The universe is a Living Presence." When regarding the body, we should keep this in mind. The body is a spiritual body, indwelt by Spirit in every cell. The body is a Living Pres-ence. When we regard it as such, we are then able to deny every sensation that seems to bring a message of distress, for we can affirm that there can be nothing but the Presence of Spirit at the very spot where something else seems to be trying to make its presence known.

Instances of healing: For many years, a woman had suffered splitting headaches. She had been told by her doctor, who happened to be a neighbor as well, that nothing could be done for migraine.

I suggested that she consider her body pure Spiritual Substance; that she reason with herself until she was convinced that Spirit could not suffer pain; and that she do this when no headache was apparent. She began to do this daily.

Instead of experiencing a recurrence every few days as she had previously, she was free of it for several weeks when, after an evening of bridge, she suffered another attack. She gave way to it for a time, then decided that the concept that had kept it away for so long should have some effect now.

She made herself as quiet as she could, for she was in great agony, and proceeded to argue with herself that there could not possibly be distress there, because right at the spot where pain seemed to be, all the fullness of God was. Quietly she kept repeating this truth, which was absolute fact, until in about twenty minutes the pain had gone. Twelve years later when she passed on, she had never had another headache. "Not by might, nor by power, but by my Spirit, saith the Lord."

Speaking of headaches—a certain young man used to have them. He had been in the habit of taking two aspirins every hour for about three hours whenever he suffered from a headache. It was the only thing he had ever found effective.

After he had been taught the truth about spiritual healing, he telephoned one day and said he had another headache and wanted to know what he should do. I told him much the same as I had told the woman in the preceding instance. He phoned again in about an hour and said it didn't work. I felt that if he could have the pain dulled down a little, his mind could be brought under better control; so I did something that would horrify some spiritual practitioners. I suggested that he take one aspirin only, and go on with his spiritual treatment. The morning after, he came to the office to report that it had worked nicely.

Sometimes one is too near to his own suffering to be able to treat himself successfully. While we know that we have a perfect Law to work for us, the suffering might be so great that we have a very imperfect consciousness. In such an event, a little material assistance might be helpful in order to lessen the distress so that the sufferer can mentally detach himself sufficiently from his feelings to gain the mental quiet that is necessary for successful treatment.

We must try to remember that since there is only One Mind, we are inheritors of the race memory. All the experiences of the race are buried in that One Mind, for nothing is ever lost. The race has had much experience of pain and sickness. Gradually in the race consciousness, pain became associated with fear, because pain was the forerunner of death. Pain and distress are, therefore, likely to shake one violently, rendering difficult his attempts to isolate himself from the fear.

Growth in spiritual consciousness: As the person develops in this new attitude toward sickness, he learns how to deal with his various difficulties. Gradually, as his consciousness clears, and his spiritual vision becomes single eyed, he finds a growing mastery over his moods, his fears, his various physical states.

One need not be discouraged if at first he does not rise to lofty heights. Many make rapid progress in the first few days and weeks as they seek this new mastery, but, occasionally, one finds some difficulty in adjusting his thought to these new concepts. He can find encouragement in the thought that progress is usually much faster than is apparent to him. The subjective mind is quite educable, and the process of re-education is going on beneath the surface every moment.

One clear idea, steadily followed, is sufficient to remake his physical condition. He should, therefore, hold steadily to his new belief, for as surely as day follows night, he will grow into a knowledge that enables him to become master of his thought instead of slave, and as his thought is healed, so does his body follow, because health is a mental as well as a physical state.

HEALTH—A LIFE AS WELL AS A BELIEF

Since we are bringing forth the facts about the spiritual activity in healing, we might go further and say that the state of health involves a life as well as a belief.

"... *the gift without the Giver. ...*": Many people make use of this belief in order to get themselves out of trouble whenever they find themselves in a tight spot. The Law of Mind operates so neutrally that whenever it is consciously directed into action, it swings its great creative power in the direction we choose; therefore, the sporadic treatments these people give for themselves, or have someone else give for them, often produce good results.

But this is the second-best way. The person living his life in this way misses much because he gets the gift without becoming acquainted with the Giver. He never comes into that delightful relationship that is called "Knowing God." He may know much about God, but the impersonal God becomes personal to the one who throws wide the whole of his being to the spiritual cultivation of the Presence of God.

While it is true that one may use this belief to get things from time to time, this occasional contact with Spirit leads to a paucity of achievement and to a lack of the deeper satisfactions of life.

"Seek first the kingdom of God. . . .": Jesus pointed this out in one of his discourses. He was surrounded by a crowd that worried whether they could use this Law to get food, clothes, and shelter. He assured them that it is quite possible to do this, but he carried their eyes higher when he showed them that while this is desirable, the highest and most satisfying life is that lived in the conscious cultivation of the Life of Spirit. And he concluded by reminding them that if they would seek first the kingdom of God and His righteousness, all these other things would automatically be theirs.

There is need today to cultivate the mode of life that in itself logically produces health and happiness.

And lest the reader should think that these words savor of preachments, may we say that we are not referring to the old evangelistic message that was summed up in the words, "Get right with God." That call usually meant that one must turn over a new leaf, give up smoking, gambling, and other undesirable activities. It was compulsory. We wish to say that there is nothing compulsory in this new larger life.

Jesus rarely discussed morals; there were thousands of teachers doing it in his day. He tried to show a life in which one's mental and spiritual vision clears, and as it clears, one senses if anything is a hindrance to him and lets it go, not because he is compelled to do so, but because he has found that the deepest joys of life are in approximating one's thought to the Thought of Spirit.

This is the mode of life that guarantees freedom from sickness.

In other words, since the Mind of God activates everything in the universe, since it holds together the atoms in this book, and keeps every blade of vegetation growing, since it controls the action of the sun which keeps this planet alive, since it digests our food and keeps our hearts pumping, since it controls the nerves so we can see, hear, and move, would it not be a good idea to spend time in finding out all we can about it, not in any ecclesiastical sense, but in order to achieve greater co-operation with it?

Since man was created as an expression of Spirit, will he not find his highest happiness when he is fulfilling the purpose for which he was created? Since the Law of the universe operates for the greatest good of everything in the universe, will he not experience his highest good by bringing his thought and actions into oneness with what he learns to be the Mind of Spirit?

These are not ecclesiastical questions. They are the kind of thing that a thinking, reasonable person would logically try to find out.

The scientist does this in his particular field. If he is to gain the co-operation of particles of matter, he must sit where he can observe them, trying to deduce the laws of their action. When he has satisfied himself as to their fundamental causes of action, he then proceeds to apply his thought to the best ways of controlling them. Thus he finds that when he co-operates with them, they in turn co-operate with him. In consequence, we have invention and progress.

The same procedure is necessary in the thought-life. The Infinite is not hiding Himself. God can be known. The only co-operation we shall ever get from God is that which grows out of our co-operating with Him, just as the material scientist does. This is what we mean by knowing God.

"THE GREATEST OF THESE . . ."

If we may carry on in a nontheological sense, we would say that there is one word used in connection with God by all those of lofty vision and great spiritual accomplishment. That word is Love. Perhaps the greatest three words ever spoken were "God is Love." Love is the very nature of God.

Love is not some slushy sentimental emotion; it is a tremendous, dynamic healing force. The whole of creation, of healing, of perfection is the outcropping of Infinite Love. Love is a creative agent. All the givingness of God is the outcome of the Love of God.

The Great Law of the universe, in which are included all the lesser laws, is merely the Love of God in action. "Love is the fulfilling of the Law." It is the one great irresistible force in the universe, which sweeps away seeming obstructions and brings health, happiness, and prosperity to every soul that opens itself up to its inflow.

Nothing integrates the character as love does. Nothing adds to the power of life as fully as love does. Love will heal any situation, any disease. Without it, one may give all his goods to the poor, may have all knowledge, may give his body to be burned, but it profiteth him nothing.

Please remember that we are talking, not about the gushy sentiment often called love, but the intense desire for the well-being of others that characterizes the nature of God. This same Love, allowed to saturate us and flow unrestrictedly out to every living soul, will break through all barriers and bring to them and to us the fulfillment of the heart's desire.

Loving versus *liking:* There is a difference between loving a person and liking him. People sometimes say, "You cannot love everyone. Some are so mean or irritating that it is impossible to love them."

Let us get our terms straight. One *likes* the exterior of a person. One *loves* the inner man. True, some people are irritating. We may not like their exterior, and we do not have to. We love a person when we wish for him all that we wish for ourself. We wish for ourself abundant health, sufficient money, and happiness within. We love our neighbor as ourself when we wish for him the same things.

We may not care for his company enough to invite him into our home, but we dare not allow that dislike of his outer to enter into our wishes for him. He may have done unscrupulous, unkind things to us, may have proved him-

self unreliable, and we cannot entrust him with those
things we value.

But even though we hold him at arm's length at those
points, we should always be careful to keep those irritating
things on the outside of us. When we allow them to get
inside, they become part of us and hurt us. When we send
out love, it nullifies all that he is. When we send out hate,
it nullifies all that God is.

We can recognize that he is Spirit at his center just as
much as we are. We love the inner spiritual man even
when we avoid the outer imperfect manifestation. We forgive the unkind things, and whenever he comes into our
consciousness, we quietly wish him all the good in the universe. We cannot claim our good and at the same time
mentally shut another away from that good.

Very often our refusal to allow his unkindness to enter
our inner consciousness, coupled with our conscious *choice*
of love toward him, is the healing force that plays upon
him and eradicates that outer imperfect man, revealing the
true man beneath.

We therefore "love our enemies." Whenever the race
thought of tit for tat comes in, we use that God-given power
of conscious *choice* to turn away from the spirit of criticism, condemnation, and anger definitely to *select* and
choose to pour our love in his direction.

He is our brother. "If a man say, 'I love God,' and hate
his brother, he is a liar," said one who knew this spiritual
universe, "for if he hate his brother whom he hath seen,
how can he love God whom he hath never seen?" That un-
likable person is an incarnation of God; therefore, we love

him because that is the only form in which we see God through these physical eyes.

A fundamental of successful spiritual treatment: One of the fundamentals of successful spiritual treatment is that we must surround each person we treat for with all our love. We can never be instrumental in healing another unless we love him much.

And if we hold back a little corner of our heart for a pet hate for *anyone,* we cannot saturate with love those whom we are trying to help, any more than we can put a drop of black ink in a pail of water and expect it to stay in the place we put it. Hate poisons, but love heals.

This is probably why Jesus, knowing the tendency of members of a group to allow their irritations to rise, used a strong word when he said, "I command you to love one another."

When we surround each person for whom we treat with our spiritual love, it is not a vaporous sentiment, but a mighty power because it is God-Power. It is as definite as a stream of water directed through a hose in a definite direction, and it washes its object clean.

POINTS FOR SPECIAL CONSIDERATION

The reader who wants to grow in spiritual consciousness and learn to use energy on its highest level, that of the spiritual, will think through the following from every point of view.

We are working with perfect Law, which knows how to heal any condition no matter how serious it may appear to be.

Mind operates creatively through a Law that is as certain as that of gravitation or electricity.

The successful practitioner must avoid both conceit and self-depreciation.

As long as one's knowledge of, and confidence in, the Power are greater than his fear of the condition, he can bring healing.

Spirit is the Eternal I AM, forever dwelling in Perfection, the true norm by which we shape our thought.

Spiritual thought-force has power over everything unlike itself.

The deepest joys of life are found in approximating one's thought to the Thought of Spirit.

Love is the intense desire for the well-being of others, a tremendous, dynamic healing force, a fundamental in successful treatment.

VIII

The Powerhouse Within Us

> To the degree that we open our whole selves to the All-Powerful Presence, and get the feel, the awareness of it, we shall have power.

We have stressed the necessity of clear knowledge of mental Law for successful healing. But in addition to clear knowledge, there must be something else. Not only what we know, but what we feel is important.

INNER, MYSTICAL, FIRSTHAND KNOWLEDGE

There is an inner knowledge, a knowledge that is not the result of intellectual processes. It is something mystical and firsthand gained directly from the Source of all knowledge.

The scientist and the philosopher arrive at truth through the colder channels of intellect and reason.

The spiritual practitioner uses both of these, but in addition he arrives at the conviction of truth through a third channel, that of immediate perception. This brings him the truth that is sensed rather than reasoned although it never violates reason. He senses the Infinite Presence pervading the entire universe including himself. He senses that Presence in every thing and in every person he meets, and this gives him a conviction of the unbreakable unity of the Whole.

The mystic arrives at truth, not through the physical senses or the intellect, but through intuition. He does not ignore or belittle the other approaches; he simply recognizes that there are different levels of approach. He attains knowledge of God and of spiritual truths by immediate intuition direct from the Source. Though he may use reason and logic in thinking about these truths, he first apprehends them in intuitive flashes.

He has learned that God is within him; that man is never alone. He has a sense of oneness with Reality.

He has learned to withdraw from the haranguing voices of men, from their false notions, their sheeplike following of commonly accepted ideas, and has gone into the deepest part of himself, there to contact the Infinite. In a sense, he has looked into the face of God, has heard things that he intuitively knows are basic truths, and has come forth to speak that which he knows of a certainty, for he has the authority of inner experience. He has brought forth knowledge that has worn well in all centuries, because it is timeless; it is never dated.

He sees beyond the commonly accepted interpretations of the universe. He might be said to have the ability to dissolves the physical, or material, universe into a spiritual universe. It might be said that he lives in the entire universe, not just his little segment of it; that he lives in all time and all space. From what he has learned comes a sense of peace and spiritual serenity far above what the ordinary person experiences.

Not alone the founders of the great religions, but every poet whose work has lasted has possessed the mystical quality. The inspired poet of the Book of Job had it. Dante wrote in *The Divine Comedy* of the inner journey that each of us makes and of "The Love that moves the sun and the other stars." "Speak to Him, thou, for He hears, and spirit with Spirit can meet / Closer is He than breathing, and nearer than hands and feet," wrote Tennyson. To Wordsworth, a little primrose on a rock seemed the court of the Deity. To Elizabeth Barrett Browning, "Earth's crowned with heaven, and every common bush afire with God." Shelley, Whitman, Blake, and every other poet whose work has endured has contacted Something beyond the physical senses and the intellect.

One senses, rather than analyzes, as he reads them, that they walk always in the shadow of a Living Presence so near that they can touch it, which they are trying to find words to express, and which as great poets they do express. Thus their readers are conscious of an indefinable something that saturates their words, a Presence whose imperturbable calm stills the soul. It might almost be called a fragrance that subtly pervades the atmosphere of their words. Its effect is felt rather than recognized.

The Reality of the Infinite Presence: This mystical knowledge stresses first of all the Reality of the Infinite Presence and the possibility of consciously cultivating it. It fills not only man, but the entire universe of mountains, rivers, trees, people, birds, butterflies. It fills even those things that man has regarded with enmity and disgust. It is in and through all things. We live in a spiritual universe, every atom of which is indwelt by the Infinite Presence.

Mystics of all ages, differing in birth and conditioning, nevertheless all tell of the oneness of everything. They see the universe as a single expression. They sense the kinship between everything, the brotherhood of all men.

The true destiny of man: Out of this perfect knowledge of the universe another concept comes. It is that the true destiny of man is to manifest mastery in all his affairs.

The average experience of the race has been that of defeat and sickness. Thus man is born with an accumulation of negative memories, which are so self-evident to the senses that we have accepted them as destiny. It has been believed for so long that it has come to be regarded as the truth, and the race labors under the delusion that man is born to sickness, sorrow, and limitation.

But it is a lie; it is a false standard of normalcy, accepted because we have looked at life through the eyes of the race.

In moments of illumination, most of us have felt that this surely could not be the intended level of life. In our deepest moments, each of us senses the real truth, which is that man is born to some higher destiny; that his normal standard of life is far higher than the race has accepted. Our lofty glimpses of spiritual and physical perfection have been so far above the false standard that we have scarcely dared to voice them.

We must dare to search for true normalcy, because we shall get only what we have mentally accepted as normal.

Not what we wish for or plead for, but only what we regard as normal shall we ever experience.

The mass has been looking through the eyes of racial experience, and that has been the limit of the heights to which it has attained. We must close our eyes to this, and look at life through the eyes of Spirit, for if we are originated from Spirit, then it follows logically that whatever Spirit is in itself, we have the right to expect we can reproduce within ourselves.

This is a high standard viewed in the light of what man has achieved; so the tendency is to shrink from it and accept the lower standard. This means stagnation. Man must live up to the highest truth he knows, not the lowest. He must go on to higher experiences; and in order to experience the fullest good, he must mentally expect the highest good as the normal level of life for him.

Jesus' teaching: There are some truths that we can know but can never prove through reasoning processes. These are what give force, weight, and conviction to our work.

When Jesus told the teachers that they were teaching what they had in turn been taught, while he was speaking what he knew and had seen, he was revealing one of the secrets of his tremendous authority over the forces of evil. He did not argue very much. He demonstrated the working of this Presence that was as truly a part of him as his own blood was, and let the results speak for themselves.

What then did he teach?

Jesus taught that there is a great indwelling Power and Intelligence that heals by the recognition of its Presence. The purpose of the practitioner is to recognize the Presence, grasp the immensity of this concept, draw it through his mind until it becomes a living reality, and recognize its operation.

Jesus knew intuitively that God and His universe are inseparable. In fact, instead of speaking of God *and* His universe, or God *and* man, or God *and* anything, he spoke of God *in* His universe, *in* man, *in* everything, through this inherent Presence. He taught that the Infinite cannot be divided against itself; it could not possibly be anything less than a single complete Whole.

Since man is a part of this Great Whole, he never is nor could be separated from God. His sicknesses are, therefore, only thoughts that have taken form and are never unchangeable realities.

He knew that God, being indivisible, must be in His totality in every man. All of God must be present at every point. Thus, whenever he spoke his word in the presence of disease, he was not bringing up one isolated soldier to rout the enemy; he was bringing up the entire army, and he knew ahead of time that victory was his because there was nothing that could stand against the Almighty Presence.

This God within was his daily associate. He walked and talked with men outwardly, but inwardly he walked and talked with the whole of the Father within. Subjected as he was to the terrific assault of the world-thought upon his mentality, he lived withdrawn in the deep centers of his being, holding his spiritual center open to the infilling Presence of Spirit, for "spirit with Spirit can meet."

He was tempted in all points like as we are, but when the pressure from without became particularly great, he went alone to a secluded place, there to recapture his clear

vision of the Presence within and of his inseparable oneness with the Father. When he returned, strong in healing
power, he explained it by simply saying, "The Father in
me, He it is that doeth the work." We repeat this verse
frequently, without apology, because it is the secret of all
healing.

Thus we are brought back once more to the fact that
healing is accomplished, not through the healer's effort,
but through allowing the truth to flow through and set
men free.

This truth of the oneness of God and man, clearly understood, heals illness by recognizing its nothingness. In
truth, we are healed of diseases we never had except in our
false belief, for God cannot be sick, and we are one with
God.

When we speak our word, Spirit speaks. We do not have
to raise our voice or force our will power in order to get
results, for all the irresistible Power of the Presence flows
immediately in the direction of the word of Spirit.

Here we have the reason why Jesus faced the leper, the
blind, the paralyzed, and commanded the condition with
authority; why he faced the maniac from whom all men
fled and brought him to the quiet of his right mind; why
he commanded the wind and the waves to allow peace to
flow through them; why he faced the crafty Pilate with
equanimity, and dwarfed him by his own poise.

He did not face situations alone. Always he had the
mystical sense of that Presence which embraces all Wisdom, Intelligence, Power, Love, Healing, Joy in the universe, and which is irresistible. "I and the Father are one."

The race blanches at the appearance of the witches,

ogres, and devils of disease. He despised these false appearances, and commanded them to disappear.

The more we develop the mystical sense of our complete oneness with this irresistible healing Presence, the
more completely will our word be accompanied by healings.

THE POWER AND WISDOM OF THE PRESENCE

When we think of the tremendous power manifested
throughout the universe, and realize that "All power is
given unto me," it shrinks seemingly big things to infinitesimal ones.

We know that our earth is a massive, weighty sphere,
huge in comparison with even our continent. It is kept
spinning regularly and moving at tremendous speed on
its orbital path by the Power and Wisdom of the Presence.

Yet out in space, ninety-three millions of miles away, is
a sun that dwarfs our planet. It is also completely subject
to this Power and Intelligence. And away out beyond our
sun are other suns, compared to which our sun is just a
tiny grain of sand, and away out into infinity this silent
worker, Intelligence, holds the entire universe in control,
whirling those massive bodies at incredible speeds through
space, at the same time pouring life and vitality into every
living thing, and still penetrating the tiniest organism with
itself.

It creates a giant sun or a microscopic bacterium with
equal ease, because it is never conscious of effort.

This is the great indwelling Intelligence, which heals by

the recognition of its presence. This is the Power that we are privileged to direct by our word.

Let us stop for a while and let this truth soak itself through and through our consciousness until the immensity of it dawns upon us. Then we shall never have to ask what to do to get faith. We shall have it in as large a measure as is our understanding of the mighty Cosmic Forces.

PRACTICING THE PRESENCE

Some things are helpful in keeping the sense of the indwelling Presence alive. Practice the Presence of God. Look for it everywhere. Recognize it. Cultivate it. The older theologies separated things into the physical world and the spiritual world. Break down this partition. Learn to see God *in* His universe.

See the Presence in the delicate coloring of a fragile flower, in its fragrance. See it in the song of the bird, in the laughter of children at play, in the antics of a kitten with a ball. See it in the intelligence that flows through the carpenter building a house, or the shoemaker at his last, or the merchant building a business. See it in a musical strain, in the ebb and flow of the tide, in the graceful arch of a swan's neck. Wherever intelligence is seen, it is the Presence.

See it in the person who disagrees with you, in the so-called ugly things of life, in the bacillus, the rattlesnake, the war monster. Know that the *intelligence* they use is that One Intelligence even though they may not be *using* it for what seems to be the good of mankind.

Learn to see God everywhere because He is everywhere; He cannot be divided. Learn to see God at the very spot where others say they see disease. Declare this Presence. It heals. It brings happiness. It harmonizes.

Nothing is impossible to the person who will assiduously practice the Presence of God in a nontheological way.

This does not mean that we become any less human, or that we give up the ordinary pleasures of life. It does not mean that we adopt a religious attitude as though the Presence were so awesome that we could not afford to forget it for a moment. On the contrary, we come to see God in every thing and in every person. We see Him in the festive gathering, in our social contacts, in the house of grief, in the sick chamber, in the place of danger, in our vacation experiences, and in our work.

The salesman calling upon his prospects, the housewife in her kitchen, the businessman in his store, the mechanic at his work, can rejoice because it is "God that worketh in them to will and to do of His good pleasure." Work is lifted from the commonplace to a new dignity. Drudgery is a thing of the past.

This change in our inner attitude will in itself harmonize our surroundings, or else it will open the way for our removal into better circumstances.

The Psalmist gave expression to this mystical sense of the inescapable Presence when he said:

Whither shall I go from thy Spirit, or whither shall I flee from thy Presence?

If I ascend up into heaven, thou art there; if I make my bed in hell, behold, thou art there.

If I take the wings of the morning, and dwell in the uttermost parts of the sea, even there shall thy hand lead me, and thy right hand shall hold me.

If I say, "Surely the darkness shall cover me," even the night shall be light about me. Yea, the darkness hideth not from thee, but the night shineth as the day. The darkness and the light are both alike to thee.

The Source of power: While the intellectual approach to the subject of healing is invaluable, we should never forget that power comes from the cultivation of the mystical. The intellectual is the outer approach to truth; the mystical is the inner. We need to develop the inner side of life.

We do this by spending time in quiet contemplation of the fact that each of us is just as truly and completely indwelt by the Infinite Presence as Jesus or any other outstanding man; that every erg of energy that was available to Jesus is available to us; that our body is so completely intertwined with this Presence that they cannot be separated; that every single cell of the body is filled to its capacity by this Presence; that God is not one inch farther away from us than He was from Jesus; that all this healing Presence, in its entirety, is in us at this very moment awaiting our recognition.

To the degree that we open our whole selves to the All-Powerful Presence, and get the feel, the awareness, of it, we shall have power.

CORRECTING A FAULTY POSITION

But suppose that in spite of our knowledge and acceptance of this fact of the indwelling Presence, some condition arises that is opposite to all this. We are learning a new Normal Standard of life. We believe in it; yet from time to time the lower level of the old standard rears its head.

Some might say we should not anticipate such things. It is not wise to avoid the issue by saying that we are thinking negatively if we consider it. This book is intended to assist the reader, not only into the new truth, but with instruction that will enable him to correct his faulty position if something should show up as a weakness.

Let us assume, therefore, that sickness or distress shows up.

Spiritual treatment: The first thing is to know that this limitation is not a part of the Infinite Plan. It is an experience of our own consciousness. It has no law to perpetuate it, for Law is working always to support the perfection of Spirit.

Then we turn completely away from any contemplation of this thing, to the contemplation of the Healing Presence within. We declare that this Presence has the only rights in our consciousness, and we welcome it. We invite it to make itself felt. We fill our consciousness with the thought of the spiritual perfection, which is the only thing that can manifest through the Spiritual Substance that is our body.

If doubts persist, we deny the Reality and the Truth of

everything that contradicts our word. We treat to know
within ourself that our word can change the appearance of
this condition.

We declare quietly that since no place was provided in
the body for such images, they must be false. They cannot
possibly have any power over us because we do not believe
in them. They are interlopers, claim-jumpers, trying to
bluff the real owner off the land; they have no rights and
no power of themselves. They have fooled the race, but
they cannot fool us into believing in their Reality. They
are bogy-men that used to scare us as a child, but now we
have arrived at spiritual maturity, we wonder why we ever
allowed them to have dominance over us. In other words,
we declare their nothingness in Reality.

We are at home in the spiritual world; therefore, we
do not allow ourself to be swept off our feet emotionally.
We calmly speak the word, knowing that it is the word of
Spirit.

We frame our statement, making it quite specific, taking
in every point that might help us see the truth and know
it.

If the heart is involved, we specifically declare that the
heart is the vehicle of Spirit, and that the healing Presence
is at that very spot at this very moment. Whatever particular organ seems to be in the picture, we mention it, praise
it, surround it with our healing love, and speak our word
for ease, harmony, proper functioning, and for the sensation of well-being.

Thus we present the picture of a pefectly harmonious
organism, the dwelling place of Spirit.

THE POWERHOUSE WITHIN US

We do not fall into the error of struggling with all our mentality to fight off the invader. On the contrary, we *release* the whole thing to the great Law of Mind, knowing that since it holds in place every huge sun and every tiny atom, it is now in control and bringing our thought about our body into manifestation. We keep our consciousness in as relaxed a state as possible in order to let Spirit flow out into manifestation. We let go, and let God do it.

MAN AS MIND

What has been said of the Allness of Mind should not cause us to think that we are nothing at all in this great healing scheme. Man not only releases his thought into Mind, but is that same Mind himself. Man is the greatest, grandest, most powerful thing in the universe.

Unless he realizes this, the vastness of the universe over-awes him. He searches away out into the seemingly un-countable trillions of miles of space, to the shores of huge heavenly bodies, and feels at times like the writer who said, "When I consider thy heavens, the work of thy fingers . . . , what is man that thou art mindful of him?"

He sees the terrific forces that are unleashed in the tornado, the earthquake, the lightning, the tides. In their presence, he seems to be but a tiny insect confronted by a prodigious elemental force, an ant clinging to a log at the foot of Niagara Falls. He comes in contact with the gross material forms of the universe, and discovers their terrifying power to crush the life out of him.

This is superficial reasoning, for man is far greater than any or all of those blind forces and forms. They may outweigh him in bulk, but he is superior to them because he is Mind.

Even before he built space ships, even while his physical make-up compelled him to stand upon this planet, his mentality enabled him to roam the universe at will. Man as Mind touches every other star, planet, and sun, compelling them to yield up their secrets. He compels them to tell him their weight and mass, their distances, the speed at which they are traveling, their gravity, atmosphere, temperature, and the possibility of life upon them. His mind roams throughout space, capturing and measuring various rays and waves.

Man delves into the mysteries of his own planet, compelling it to tell him how fast it is carrying him through space and the length of its orbit. His mind places the age-old rock in his test tube and searches out its constituent elements. He divides and subdivides the planet down to the smallest possible particle, and asks, "What are you?" It divulges the information that, although hard and solid in the mass, it is in reality force trapped as vibration.

These material forms and forces have no power to understand him; but he, as a mentality, has very complete knowledge of them. They are subject to the simple laws of the universe of which they are a part, but he has discovered higher laws that transcend them.

He is, therefore, able to send material forms in a direction in which they themselves have no power to travel. A piece of metal dropping from a cliff is drawn to the bottom through the operation of the law of gravitation. Man takes that metal and, by the application of other principles of physics, flies through the air upon it.

The granite boulder can crush the physical frame of man, but the mind of man can shatter the boulder by means of an explosive. The mind of man can pierce steel and the hardest of all substances, the diamond; it can put hundreds of holes in the head of a pin; it can vaporize any substance at close range—all this by means of the fantastic light of the laser beam.

Air-breathing animals can remain under water only so long as the air in their lungs holds out. The mind of man enables him to circumnavigate the globe under water, to stay submerged for a year, to live comfortably for extended periods in a sea laboratory hundreds of feet below the surface where he can study an underwater world of beauty and mystery.

The mind of man has created a spaceship of literally millions of parts, with back-up systems and built-in safety features so there will be no weak spots and all parts function in perfect interaction. He has built the giant Saturn rocket to generate the speed of about twenty-five thousand miles an hour necessary to free his spaceship from earth's gravity and carry it the quarter of a million miles to the moon and bring it back again.

The mind of man has created computers to do the prodigious amount of calculating necessary for the construction, launching, guiding, and landing of his space vehicles. How exact and precise those elaborate mathematical computations are is evidenced in the launching of Apollo 11 only 724 milliseconds—724/1000 of a second—off the scheduled time.

The mind of man has created computers to be electronic tellers in banking institutions; to be supervisors in factories; to be warehouse managers, moving in and storing a product in the right place and moving it out in the kind and quantity ordered; to sort out traffic at airports; to prepare payrolls and statements; to store vast quantities of information; to teach; to translate; to analyze; to predict. The speed of some of their operations is reckoned in billionths of a second.

But the computer is not a mind; it is only a mechanical brain. It was made by the mind of man.

The mind of man has constructed the 200-inch Mt. Palomar telescope which increases his visual range so greatly that it has brought within his vision a galaxy 5,000,000,000 light-years away. The light by which the astronomer sees that galaxy left it *5,000,000,000 years ago,* and has been traveling *186,000 miles a second* ever since that time. Yet the greatest thing about that giant telescope and the galaxies it sees is the mind behind the eye that looks through it at them. "In the last analysis," said Dr. Raymond B. Fosdick, "the mind which encompasses the universe is more marvelous than the universe which encompasses the mind."

Man has built granite monuments, steel battleships, towering skyscrapers, that will physically outlast him; yet he is greater than all these because he is Mind.

In his primitive days, man fled from the lightning and hid his face in fear. But when he became a thinker, he studied the lightning fearlessly, then went into the laboratory and produced a lightning bolt of millions of volts of electricity.

Formerly, he worshiped the sun as a god who brought him life and health. Now, he separates its various rays, goes into his laboratory and makes an ultraviolet lamp which is his indoor sun when the clouds overcast the heavens.

Man can carve his inmost thoughts on stone, or set them down in black scratches on papyrus or paper, or record them on wax or tape. Thousands of years later, his mind can communicate through these words with the minds of men who read or hear what he has written or spoken. Thus man, being Mind, is eternal, and "He, being dead, yet speaketh." As Lytton Strachey said, "Perhaps of all the creations of man, language is the most astonishing."

Man may appear tiny, puny, and insignificant in the midst of forces so great; but he is a mind, and as a mind he is greater and more powerful than anything he touches.

Man, as Mind, has been able to search his way back across the long succession of ages, stretching away back into timeless antiquity, and has found out the way in which he believes this physical universe had its origin. He has discovered that the materials of which it is composed are blind, unmoving, having no power to originate action or life within themselves. He has learned that they are forever acted upon and moved by Mind, and that since he is one with the One Mind, he is master of all he surveys.

THE BALANCE

We need to maintain a balance between a confident appraisal of our personal value in the universe, of our own mental dominance, on the one hand, and, on the other hand, of our absolute dependence upon Cosmic Mind. As we balance these two, we are kept humble yet confident, which is the proper attitude of the person who would be successful in applying the healing Principle.

"Let this Mind be in you, which was also in Christ Jesus, who, being in the form of God, thought it not robbery to be equal with God, but made himself of no reputation, and took upon himself the form of a servant."

We take the stand that man has proved his spiritual origin and that of the universe, and we proceed upon the assumption that Spirit is the directive Cause of all the activity of Mind. Consequently, all creative activity is, in the final analysis, spiritual. Innumerable observations and the conclusions drawn from them bear out the assumption that Spirit is the moving force of the universe, and that Spirit always acts through intelligent law to produce material forms.

Many of these observations and conclusions have been in the field of sickness and health, in which correctly diagnosed physical maladies were changed into a condition in which there was no further sign of disease. The disease-picture was changed in Mind to a health-picture, and yielded its ground under the influence of mental activity, which, in turn, was directed by Spirit.

It is now a proved fact that man controls substance because he is a thinker. The material scientist has searched and has discovered the laws that govern material structure. Thus he governs the behavior of the material itself so that he can produce forms through following the laws of matter.

The spiritual scientist has devoted his attention to spiritual and mental law, and demonstrates that he is able to govern the behavior of his own body and that of others by the application of that Law which terminates in healing.

One weakness of the material scientist is that he sometimes refuses to accept a spiritual conclusion unless it is based upon physical research. He has set up standards, rightfully, by which he can test and prove or disprove his theories concerning the material universe.

On the other hand, spiritual and mental theories cannot be tested by mere material standards and checks, for they must be judged and measured by spiritual and mental standards. Hence, when a material scientist denies the conclusions of mental and spiritual science on the grounds that they cannot be proved by his particular yardstick, he is like the man who refuses to measure the air because all he has is a foot rule.

POINTS FOR SPECIAL CONSIDERATION

The reader who wants to learn to use the power within him will give careful attention to the following.

When we think of the tremendous power manifested throughout the universe, and realize that "All power is given unto me," it shrinks big things to infinitesimal ones.

Practice the Presence. Look for it everywhere. Recognize it. Cultivate it.

Learn to see God at the very spot where others say they see illness.

Nothing is impossible to the person who will assiduously practice the Presence of God in a nontheological way.

All the healing Presence, in its entirety, is in us at this very moment, awaiting our recognition.

Man is superior to all the blind forces and forms of the universe, for he is Mind.

We need to maintain a balance between a confident appraisal of our personal value in the universe, of our own mental dominance on the one hand; and, on the other, of our absolute dependence upon Cosmic Mind.

CHAPTER IX

Actual Cases of Healing

> We can never manifest a desirable physical state while entertaining an undesirable mental state.

It might be well to turn from the theory of healing to the practical aspects. Following are a few cases that were treated, and the exact steps followed in each case.

There is no magic power in words of themselves. The mere repetition of words used in another healing is useless. One must invest those words with the proper thought. It is thought that heals. An entirely different form of words might be used in the same kind of treatment, and those words would be powerful because the thought that gave rise to them was clear and powerful.

These healing treatments are therefore not given as those to be slavishly followed in similar cases, but they will be valuable as a guide. The reader can watch the way these people treated themselves, and conform his *method* to that used successfully in these cases.

The identity of the persons involved is protected by the use of fictitious names.

ECZEMATOUS RASH

Mrs. Hill was a widow with an eczematous rash on head and body for several years. She had gone to various hot springs, and had used salves and ointments, in addition to having been treated by both medical and drugless methods.

During our conversation, it developed that there was much friction between her and a cousin who had lived with her for fifteen years. Finally, they had gone their separate ways, but there was much buried animosity. The mere thought of the cousin would cause considerable bitterness of mind.

I pointed out to Mrs. Hill that it was necessary that she eliminate the bitterness and irritation engendered by the thoughts of the cousin. She was unwilling to do this. I told her rather firmly that it would be futile for her to expect healing unless she was willing to "forgive her debtor."

Jesus brought this out on several occasions. "Forgive us our debts as we forgive our debtors" in the Lord's Prayer is not for eternal forgiveness of theoretical sin. He referred to a fundamental principle: that any grudge held within the heart automatically shuts off the manifestation of spiritual perfection. This is why bitterness allowed to remain in the thought-life has often wrecked the ability of a salesman or ruined a businessman, as well as affecting the health of a person.

Finally, Mrs. Hill was willing to place herself in the position of Spirit, which condemns nobody. She did not accomplish this in a moment. It was two months before she returned and said she could see the foolishness of her attitude. Then I suggested the following method of treatment. She spoke it quietly three times daily after fifteen minutes of reading and meditation upon spiritual things.

"I, Mary Hill, am surrounded by Universal Subjective Mind. My cousin, Jane Jones, is also surrounded by this Mind. We are both thinking in it and with it at this moment.

"There cannot be two hostile thought-currents in this One Mind. I speak this word, which is the Law unto my mental state, that in Mind there is but one peaceful condition; that my cousin and I are both completely at peace in that Mind. I forgive myself and her for our blindness in thus raising an inharmony that was not there in the first place. I completely eliminate and erase and dissolve all sense of hurt, all anger, all irritation.

"There is nothing anywhere that has the power to irritate me, because I dwell in the eternal calm of Spirit. I am the embodiment of Spirit, which dispenses nothing but peace, harmony, perfection.

"I embrace Janes Jones and surround her with my deepest and warmest love. I surround all persons with the same divinely inspired love.

"I speak my word for the complete removal of all sense of irritation concerning anything anywhere in my world, and send forth my peace to surround everything with which I come in contact.

"My body is Spiritual Substance, and cannot be limited by anything that irritates. My skin is the dwelling place of Spirit, and knows only peace, smoothness, and fineness. I now direct the Law of Mind to manifest in my mental states and in my body and my skin that spiritual perfection which is always the state of Spirit.

"I now consciously deliver this body over to the perfect working of perfect Law according to this my word of perfection.

"And I rejoice in its perfect fulfillment because I know that it is done as I say even now."

In a few weeks, the eczema had completely disappeared, and has never returned.

When Jesus told his audience that if they came bringing their gift to the altar and remembered that there was hard feeling between them and another they should leave the gift, become reconciled to the brother, then come and offer their gift, he was teaching fundamental spiritual Law.

It is not always necessary personally to contact the brother and make it right. This is a good thing to do if it is feasible, but the chief thing is to get right within oneself with him, to erase the bitterness on our side and within our mental states.

It is not that God looks down and says, "That is good; now I will heal," but that it re-establishes us mentally in the universal Harmony, which is the only state of mind in which spiritual perfection can be manifested. We can never manifest a desirable physical state while entertaining an undesirable mental state. We must bring our mental state into harmony with the physical state we want to manifest.

SINUS TROUBLE

Mr. Smith had had sinus trouble since he was in high school. He had had the sinuses drained, had used atomizers containing everything from soda and water to ephedrine.

An interview brought out that he chafed under the discipline of his superior at the office. During his school days, he had felt that the football coach "had it in" for him, discriminating against him and belittling his ability as an athlete. His mental condition was what a psychologist would call a "persecution complex."

I showed him that in all probability these persons had not taken any personal pleasure out of baiting him; that there is always a need for kindly correction; that the pointing out of elements of weakness is a service for which we should feel grateful, because another can always see in us those faults that are so much a part of us that we do not notice them. We should therefore assume that the person in authority makes them for the purpose of causing us to be more efficient, and not in order to gloat over us.

But even if someone did wish to hurt us, he never can until we accept the hurt. The hurt is never in the power of another to inflict. It occurs when we wince and think, "That was intended for me, and it was a mean thing to do."

Doubtless every day that we live, someone who knows us dislikes us and says something unkind about us. But if we never hear of it, there is no hurt, which proves that the words or thoughts of others, in themselves, have no power over our happiness. If a thing was said several weeks ago, and we have not felt unhappy since then, why should we then embrace the thing the moment it is brought to our attention? We are the only persons with power to hurt ourselves by our own mental *reaction* to things said or done.

Would it not be much better for us to take this attitude: "If he really means to hurt me by this thing, I refuse to accept it; and if he didn't mean to hurt me, why should I accept it as hurtful?"

Now for the connection between the sinus trouble and the mental state: Irritated feelings leading to restricted action, in both high school and office, were probably reflected in irritation of the sinuses, leading to blocking of nasal passages.

The following suggestions for treatment were followed, and recovery resulted.

"I, John Smith, am a complete and free expression of Spirit. I was brought into the world with the birthright of growth and ever larger expression.

"Everything in the universe is likewise an expression of Spirit. Each expression is seeking larger freedom, and I treat myself to know that Spirit is granting to every other form greater freedom and growth.

"I therefore know that nothing wishes to limit me. Every person with whom I have ever been connected knows my truth worth, and wishes me to express that worth.

"I treat myself to know that nothing in the universe could confine me even if it wanted to. I know that I have at this moment all the freedom that I *choose* to exercise. I now consciously wipe out of my thought any belief in the desire of anyone or anything to block me.

"I treat myself to know that Spirit, knowing no restriction itself, is flowing through my thought and through every cell of my body at this moment.

"I rejoice at the thought that there is unlimited freedom for me—in my thought-life, in my feelings, in my entire body, and particularly in my sinuses and nasal passages. I declare it and decree it.

"And I turn this certainty over to my Servant, Universal Subjective Mind, fully expecting to see it manifest in me this perfect freedom that I know I have.

"And I grant to every other person the same freedom that I have, particularly my superior, Albert Brown, and my former coach, Sam Green."

Restriction or blockage in any part of the body is usually associated with a similar idea in the thought-life. We must be honest with ourselves in order to free ourselves from the limiting thought, for it is always the thought that restricts us first. The physical manifestation of that thought appears later. To clear the physical, we must therefore clear the mental.

IMPAIRMENT OF BODILY FUNCTION

Angus MacTavish had been an engineer on Britsh steamers, but had finally settled in the United States. Shortly after he retired he began to notice his legs trembling. Finally, he lost the power of locomotion, and had to take to a wheel-chair.

It developed that in his boyhood in Scotland there was an old seafaring man who was paralyzed, and who had to be pushed around in a rough contrivance. The boy, in the full life and energy of youth, used to shudder at the thought of such helplessness. Sometimes out of pity for the man he would take him out for an airing. Evidently the repeated sight of the old man's helplessness, and his own strong emotional reaction to it, made a deep subjective impression upon him.

The years passed, and the rough, tough life on the high seas soon caused him to forget the aged cripple. But we never forget anything that we have seen or heard. It is crowded out of the objective mind by other pictures, but it is stored in the vast depths of the subjective mind; and in this case it was a dominant thread in the subjective thought-pattern upon which the Law of Mind worked, finally producing in him, when he had reached the age of the old paralytic, a similar manifestation. "That which I greatly feared has come upon me."

Since it was an unnoticed thought that had been working, we decided that he should definitely and consciously feed into the loom of Mind the threads of the opposite picture. He began to call into Mind the memory of the old sailor, but not as he had appeared in MacTavish's youth; he definitely began to see him as a tough, weathered old salt, tramping his native heath and recounting stories of wild days at sea.

Whenever he found the old youthful horror creeping in, he would laugh at it, and say that the old sailor was the most active fellow for his age that he had ever seen, thus attacking the old fear association in his own mind. Then he would see himself and the old sailor sharing the same boundless vitality and activity of Spirit.

The form of treatment follows. He used it three times daily, each treatment being given as though it were the only one to be given—each treatment complete in itself.

"I, Angus MacTavish, am one with all the life and vitality of the universe. I rejoice in the present possession of that strength. It flowed for me in youth; it flowed for me in gales at sea; it flows for me and through me at this moment. I see all men saturated with those currents of spiritual flow.

"Nothing could ever deplete that inexhaustible store. Weakness in any part of the body is only an illusion of the *senses,* and the Law of the Spirit of Life has set me free from the apparent law of sin and death.

"I now treat myself to erase and blot out all images of weakness and helplessness anywhere in the universe and in me. I deny the reality of my picture of helplessness formed in my youth and held in subjective mind. I consciously *choose* to know that they are false, and that the truth of my perfect being now sets me free from any false belief.

"I believe in Perfect God, Perfect Man, Perfect Being, and know deep within myself that nothing unlike this has any power to manifest in my experience. I know now that the perfection of Spirit is seeking to show forth in me, and I remove all obstructing thoughts and step aside to let that perfection appear.

"This is not my will power by which it is accomplished. Not my will, but 'thine be done.' I let the perfect will of God have its perfect way in my entire body—in my brain, in my spinal cord, and in all the nerves that control the activity of my legs. I speak this my word for complete activity.

"And I release it to the perfect Law of Mind, my Servant, to carry it out. I know that it is done, and that my word shall not return to me void. It shall accomplish that whereto I have sent it."

He gradually regained the use of his legs, planted and worked in his own garden, and made a remarkable recovery over a period of years.

Why are healings not always instantaneous? Fear states cling tenaciously to man. Often it take a person some time completely to obliterate them.

The theorist sometimes asks, "Why should it not be done instantly?" The answer is that it could be done instantly if the consciousness were always perfect. But Mind works habitually, and the person who takes longer to change the mental habits of a lifetime should be encouraged to continue, rather than to be cast down by being told that God can work instantly. In the latter event, he treats once or is treated by a practitioner once, then gives up because his healing is not instantaneous.

From God's side, every healing is instantaneous. From man's side, time often elapses because of the beclouded consciousness that becomes dimly aware of truth, and that persistently follows the gleam of light until it stands in the sunlight of midday.

Everyone who is at home in the mental and spiritual world has seen numerous cases of instantaneous healing. It is better, however, to present cases where time elapsed in order to encourage the beginner that he be "not weary in welldoing, for in due season we shall reap if we faint not." Hence the preceding instances.

HEART TROUBLE

Mrs. Bell had been told that she might drop off at any moment on account of her heart. She was well along in years.

One day, sitting in her little apartment, she felt herself slipping. The cries of children playing on an adjacent vacant lot seemed to be fading away; the song of the two canaries in her apartment was becoming indistinct; everything was growing dark. She thought, "Is this the end?" Then she pulled her thoughts together and said something like this:

"God is all there is; there is nothing but Spirit, and I am Spirit. My heart is the heart of Spirit; my body is the Body of Spirit. Peace, my heart, be calm."

The attack passed. This was one of those quick treatments that are available to us in an emergency. An even shorter one is, "God is. There is nothing but God." Peter's "Lord save me" was enough at his time of emergency.

STOMACH ULCER

John White had a stomach ulcer according to an X-ray diagnosis, and suffered excruciating pains unless he remained upon an almost liquid diet.

The treatment was along this line:

"I, John White, know that I could not feel distress unless my mind told me of it. Under an anesthetic, it would be impossible for me to experience pain.

"I therefore deny that there is any distress of any sort because there is nothing in my body that could possibly cause distress. I am whole with the wholeness of Spirit; my stomach is the abode of Spirit; it is Spiritual Substance brought down to tangible form, but it is alive with the aliveness of Spirit, and since Spirit could not possibly feel pain, it feels none.

"It feels the full indwelling Presence of Spirit. It is in a perfect state. Nothing less than this has any power to operate through me, nor to manifest in me. I do not believe in it because I believe the only Reality is Spirit.

"I speak my word, which is the law unto my body, for complete wholeness, not by might, nor by power, but by my Spirit, saith the Lord. Infinite perfection, stand forth in my entire body and in my stomach now through that perfect Law."

His healing was instantaneous. He went out and enjoyed a steak dinner, and ate anything he wished thereafter.

INFLAMMATION AND SWELLING

A child's knee had been badly inflamed for weeks. It was badly swollen, and the cords were drawn so that the leg could not be straightened or bent.

The treatment, which produced instantaneous healing, consisted of only ten words: "The healing Presence of Spirit is in this knee now." This was repeated quietly a few times. The child did not hear the words, for they were repeated inaudibly.

The leg relaxed, straightened, and the pain left immediately. The crying of the child ceased, and five minutes later it was in the yard playing.

Not words but consciousness: Once more should the fact be stressed that it is not so much the form of words, but the consciousness of the one treating, that is the important thing. There must be a steady, undivided consciousness of the present perfection of the one for whom the treatment is given. The false appearance of disease must be steadily denied. There must be the faith that the Law of Mind is mighty enough to encompass anything. There must be a definite transference of the actual work to the Cosmic Intelligence.

If any doubt lingers in the consciousness of the one treating, it must be dismissed. This is usually best done through argument within oneself, designed to support the word that is spoken, and to come into a spiritual realization of the fact that this concept of the spiritual and physical perfection of the individual is now an accomplished fact.

As one gains experience, his faith grows. At first, one does not always have success in his treatment because fear is still struggling with his new faith. But as he goes along, and experience follows experience, he comes to have the conviction within himself that his treatment is an actual thing. It is a *definite movement of Mind*. The results prove it because they are far beyond what the human will could possibly produce.

To offset possible discouragement in the beginner, let it be said that frequently the best treatment ever given is the first one, given when he is in the swaddling clothes of his new belief. One does not necessarily have to bungle his way along, hoping that one day his treatment will heal.

TUBERCULOSIS

The first treatment I ever gave in behalf of another person, more than fifty years ago when I was an infant in this knowledge, resulted in an instantaneous healing of a tubercular man who had been told he had less than one lung left.

Occasionally now, when I have not been satisfied with the result of a certain treatment, I have sought to return to that particular consciousness that I must have had at that moment.

DIABETES

In my own case, when laboratory diagnosis revealed that I was suffering from diabetes, I was introduced to this thought through Judge Thomas Troward's *The Creative Process in the Individual.* I knew no one who believed in this philosophy; therefore, I had to grope my own way along the trail.

It took some years to come to the point of complete surrender to the flow of Mind, not because I was consciously obstructing, but because the thought was so foreign to what I had been trained to believe that I missed the point repeatedly. Yet there must have been some glimmer of truth in everything I did because there was some improvement right from the start.

Laboratory analysis was used to check the results week by week. Sometimes the test would show marked improvement; then for some reason, unknown to me, the quantity of sugar revealed by the test would be quite high. This went on during the entire time I was treating for myself, but gradually the trend was toward normal manifestation.

Presumably this was due to a gradually rising consciousness and clearer understanding on my part, resulting in a more complete releasing of the whole work to the Law of Mind. Now for about fifty years, I have eaten anything sugary I wish with no recurrence of the disorder.

This personal experience is interjected at this point for the sole purpose of giving courage to anyone else who may find himself in a similar position. If one cannot have the immediate perfect demonstration, he should press on courageously, knowing that he is on the right track, and that it will eventually lead him home.

Raising the consciousness: Our past life may have been very largely a discussion of friends who are sick, and of loved ones who have passed on. Until we check and analyze our thoughts, we may not notice how much we fill our consciousness with the sickness idea.

It is a wise thing, especially during the early days, to avoid the company of those people whose chief topic of conversation is sickness and funerals. This is not snobbishness; it is self-protection. Many people studiously avoid the company of the person whom they believe to have smallpox. Why should not we avoid the company of those who are mentally infected? They are more to be avoided than those having the appearance of smallpox.

—see perfection everywhere: It is good practice to see perfection wherever one goes. As we pass along the streets and see those of whom we formerly spoke as blind, deaf, crippled, and so on, we should look right at them and deny the appearance. We should do it as an exercise in looking *through* to the perfect man within. We can refuse to accept the world's decision regarding them. We can announce to ourselves the spiritual standard.

As we cultivate the habit of refusing to see the ugliness and the deformity, and use our spiritual eyesight to see *through* to the perfection, our very effort is a treatment for each one we thus envisage. So it is not just a selfish practice on our part for the purpose of developing spiritual muscle. It is partly that, but it is a benefit to them, for every thought of ours is received by Mind and acted upon.

There are persons whose very presence has a healing effect. They are those who persistently practice seeing the perfection of Spirit in everything, even in those whom the world calls lame or ill.

If there have been points of irritation in our own environment, we should make it a practice to look at those very points with a new vision. We should practice knowing within ourselves, deep within our own consciousness, that there is no irritation. The outer appearance of it may still be there, but man looketh upon the outward appearance, while the God-man looketh upon the heart.

When we learn to see in everything the picture that God sees, we are nearer Reality than those who see the opposite, for they are still living in the world of the senses, while we have gone to the heart of Reality. Then when the time comes to treat for a condition, we do not have to snatch ourselves out of a negative attitude and endeavor to lift ourselves into the place of spiritual vision.

—abide in the Vine: It is not reasonable to suppose that we can fill and surround ourselves with thoughts and words of disease, strife, disgust, poverty, envy, criticism, jealousy, and greed for twenty-three and a half hours a day, and then for the other half hour try to benefit by spiritual Law.

When Jesus told the disciples that they could not bear fruit unless they abode in the Vine, he was stating this principle. It is the steady, continuous abiding in the Vine that enables the life-giving sap to flow in the quantities necessary for the bearing of much fruit. Little abiding, little fruit. Much abiding, much fruit.

This does not mean that one need become discouraged at his failure to abide in the Vine. All of us find ourselves at times far from this consciousness of abiding. But we should make a deliberate effort to fill the consciousness with thoughts of perfection as far as possible. We should try to reverse our previous attitudes and deliberately see perfection in others whether their deformity is of the body or of the character.

—*cultivate the spirit of love:* For this reason, there should be the conscious cultivation of the spirit of love for those who are different from us, or who differ with us. Nothing kills the healing consciousness so easily as the habit of criticism. Criticism is a mild form of hate, and sometimes it is not such a mild form either.

It would be a wise move upon the part of the beginner if he were to take the stand that he would absolutely refrain from criticizing anyone no matter how much the criticism might appear to be justified. The times when it might be justified are so few in contrast to the great number of times when it is unjustified that he will not have lost anything by his restraint. On the contrary, this practice will develop within him a spiritual state that is mighty to heal.

This is the most practical suggestion so far made in this book. The person with much less technical knowledge of healing, but with much love for everyone he meets, will heal more often than the one who "has all knowledge but has not charity."

Even from a spiritually selfish standpoint, we should

bathe ourself in love, and dispense love to all we meet. We should never mention it, for there is nothing quite so saccharine as the person who is always assuring people how much he loves everybody. But we should studiously cultivate the art of loving people clear down to our depths.

Love never criticizes. Criticism poisons, but love heals.

Let it not be thought that this is a preachment. The saddest memories I have are those of my times of criticisms of others. I would dearly like to say that for fifty years I have never allowed a word of criticism to pass my lips. I would be guilty of dishonesty if I should say such a thing, but I am frankly admitting that I would be better able to heal instantaneously today if I could truthfully make such a statement. It is with chagrin that I say, "Don't do as I have done. Do as I say."

The desirable thing about following this advice is that even though one should initiate this procedure in order that he might become more successful in treating, he will eventually get beyond this idea. He will find that it smooths his path, and make his relations with everybody more pleasant. In fact, it will do more for him than it does for others, because it will bring him to the place in life where he experiences the deepest peace and harmony within himself, and where joy, like an everflowing stream, bubbles up from within his depths.

That is the joy that possessions can never give, nor their lack take away. It is the ultimate purpose of living.

POINTS FOR SPECIAL CONSIDERATION

The reader who wants to go on into the practical aspects of healing and the actual giving of treatment will dwell on the thoughts below.

The mere repetition of words used in another healing is useless. One must invest those words with the proper thought.

Spirit condemns nobody.

There cannot be two hostile thought-currents in the One Mind.

Each person is a free expression of Spirit with the birthright of growth and ever larger expression.

Each person is one with all the inexhaustible store of the life and vitality of the universe.

God is. There is nothing but God.

The healing Presence of Spirit is in this place *now*.

See perfection everywhere.

"Abide in the Vine."

Cultivate the spirit of love.

Healing and Religion

> At this very moment, there is latent in every person
> enough of the Power of God to transform him and lift
> him entirely out of his difficulty.

Mental and spiritual healing is by no means the exclusive
possession of religion. Some people object when the subject
is allied too closely to the teaching of Jesus, or when Bible
quotations are introduced to illustrate a point. The careful
reader will notice, however, that such quotations are never
introduced with the intention of bringing forth a religious
idea; they are brought in to show how body, mind, and
spirit interact.

A MASTER OF HEALING SCIENCE

Jesus came teaching man how to awaken to the fact that
disease has no power because it is not in the Infinite Plan.
His teachings have become twisted around to the point

182

where today they are chiefly used to impose moral and religious sanctions.

He was a practical teacher of the most practical truth ever taught. In fact, the religionists of his day bitterly opposed him. We therefore quote him as a master of healing science rather than as a religious authority although he was both.

We often quote from the Bible because it is the best-known book in practically every country in the world. Most of us were brought up to know it. We could quote from other literature if it were as well known.

LIGHT FROM OTHER LAMPS

The writings of India are full of mental healing. The literature of Buddhism drops this pointed word of power:

All that we are is the result of what we have thought. It is founded upon our thoughts. It is made up of our thoughts.

Again:

Just as a chariot wheel in rolling rolls only at one point of the rim, and in resting rests only at one point, so in exactly the same way the life of a living being lasts only for the period of one thought. As soon as that thought is ended, that living being is said to have ceased.

Still again:

What a man thinks, that he is. This is the ancient secret.

Buddha taught the Law of Karma, or Cause and Effect. He taught that the cause can as little evade its consequence as a man can escape his shadow. He taught that the Law of Cause and Effect is as real an energy as that which guides the sun, and streams from the sun; that it is mechanical in its working, but is generated by Intelligence. He taught that it operates only in the world of appearances; that it cannot affect the eternal, spiritual man; that when man sees his inseparable oneness with the universe and with the unchanging First Cause, he comes to reflect that First Cause in the perfection in his body.

He taught that each man is free; that he is the maker of his own destiny through his choices; but that in making his choice, he must be willing to accept the consequence that lies within it.

Plato, the Epicureans, the Stoics—all taught that inner mental states are reflected in the outer physical states. They stressed the fact that the inner life is the originating point of sickness or health.

The philosopher Plotinus followed this truth, and was able in numerous instances to heal those who came to him. Neo-Platonism, which has survived largely through his influence, is rich material for the student of mental and spiritual healing.

Spinoza, Kant, Descartes, Hegel, and Swedenborg among the philosophers and scientists all went more or less deeply into the fact that sickness and health both originate in the thought-life.

I suggest that the investigator pursue his studies further in the writings of these men and others of this age and of the past. By doing so, he will find that this is no new truth that we are proclaiming. As long as man has been a thinker, his thought has turned to the question of his health since it is the closest experience of life; and the clearest thinkers have always been brought eventually face to face with the self-evident truth that man's inward states influence his outward conditions.

THE CAUSES

The real problem has always been to probe one's way to the causative factors—the hidden underlying causes of disease that lie buried deeply in the vaults of man's consciousness.

In different ages, men have approached the problem from different angles, and different men in any one age have taken different paths in their search for the true causation; but it is a remarkable fact that each has finally arrived at the place where he has seen that either man controls his mental states or they control him. When they control him, he is the slave of circumstances and conditions; when he controls them, he is the master.

THE METHODS

In the twentieth century, there are numerous mental workers using various methods of mental analysis and mental healing. But they all fall into one of two groups, characterized by their particular method of working.

The mental: One method is that used by the psychologist, the psychiatrist, the psychosomaticist, the hypnotist, the mental suggestionist, the magnetist. Analysis and suggestion are the basis of their work. They recognize that the thought of the person has power, and they treat him from a mental point of view. For the most part, they work without any recognition of the spiritual element, but occasionally one rises to a truly spiritual level.

The mental plus the spiritual: The other method is that outlined in this book. It is the method that Jesus used, hence our frequent reference to him and his teaching.

The unbreakable unity of God in His universe is the basis of our work. Man is a spiritual being; his body is Spiritual Substance; as such, it never has been sick because Spirit could not be sick. We admit that man feels pain, suffers disease and distress as an experience, but affirm that these manifestations are merely reflections of his mental states. Basically, they have no enduring reality. In our work, we seek to realize the Infinite Mind, and constantly turn in our mind to God.

When we face the sick person, whether it be ourself or another, we turn in mind immediately to God, to perfection, and endeavor to convince ourself that this is the real state of the person before us. While we work, our thought is upon the Eternal Perfection, the spiritual world, the love, peace, harmony, joy, well-being, beauty, and power of God until we can see all these qualities reflected in this person.

Were we to drop to a lower level by filling ourself with the thought of disease, and the physical man before us with all its appearance of imperfection, we should not be using the true scientific method that Jesus used. And since he produced the best results of any healer who ever lived, we feel that his method must be nearer to the actual truth.

We have accepted the fact that our inner thought certainly has an outward corresponding effect; therefore, just as a low thought will produce a low effect, a high thought will produce a high effect; therefore, the highest thought we can entertain must have the highest possible effect. The highest thought that man can exercise is the thought of God and His perfection.

Then we bring our thought to the person for whom we are treating, and endeavor to realize deep within ourself that this one is a fragment of God, to speak rather loosely, and as such he shares all the perfection that God is. We look steadily at him, knowing within ourself that there is really nothing to heal but a false belief; that all that is needed is for his inborn spiritual perfection to manifest throughout his body and particularly at the place where his pathological condition appears to be focalized.

This does not mean that we merely say, "This person is in the image and likeness of God; therefore, he is perfect." There is much more to it than that.

We have actually to convince ourself of that fact so that it becomes a deep inward conviction that no outward appearance can shake. That God is in this person must be more than a verbal statement to us. It must become a living fact, more real than his sick appearance. As we discussed in the chapter on the method of treating, we may have to argue within ourself until this becomes absolute truth to us.

Finally, when there is no longer anything in our consciousness that denies the truth that we have uttered, we turn our perfected thought over to Universal Mind, knowing that its great creative energy is now pouring through that thought and reflecting that perfect thought in perfect form.

—*practical proof:* Is it possible for human beings, subject to all the frailties that result from their own beclouded vision, thus to rise above the world and its influence so that they can perfect their thought and see that thought reflected in healed bodies, prosperous businesses, and happy surroundings?

It certainly is! It is being done every day in every country of the world. At the moment you are reading these pages, someone is setting the Law of Mind into action for some fettered body and seeing the fetters broken.

This method of handling the problem of sickness is spreading, growing every day. No longer is it fashionable to sneer at it since someone in the company is almost certain to have been thus healed or to know someone who has.

—*scientific foundations:* The spiritual method is a scientific method. No one need stand abashed when it is mentioned, for every scientific discovery that comes from the laboratory is placing further foundations under this truth.

Scientists are delving deeper into the workings of the human mind, and are discovering that their conclusions, stated in scientific terms, coincide with the truth uttered by a carpenter in Palestine twenty centuries ago.

Physicists are probing into the structure of the atom, and as discovery after discovery comes tumbling out in rapid succession, they are coming to see that the powerhouse of the universe is not only away out in the interstellar spaces, but in the cavernous depths of the atom.

More than a hundred years ago, with science still in its infancy, Carlyle spoke these words in a flash of illumination: "Force, force, everywhere force; we ourselves are a mysterious force. There is not a leaf rotting on the highway but has force in it."

What an essay he could have written today, as he would if he could stand besides the giant cyclotron, or atom-smasher, and see the evidence piling up to prove that the infinitesimal atom is a vast abyss, in whose atomic depths are surges of energy beyond comprehension, where the dynamos of the universe ceaselessly whir, and from whose depths some day will be drawn the power to run every machine, to turn every wheel upon the earth.

THE POWER

What is this power, this energy toward which man is thus groping his dimly lit way? It is Infinite Intelligence, the identical Power that we make use of in healing.

We are using a Power that we do not fully understand. But we have learned one thing about it, which is that it flows in the direction that man's mind indicates. It is not necessary to understand the nature of radio in order to make use of it. Electricity flows for us whether we are electricians or not, and this great, throbbing, pulsating Cosmic Energy is ours for the using.

Thus the mental and spiritual healer is able to demonstrate results that often amaze the materialist, *because we are dealing with First Cause.* If our work were dependent upon us alone, then the question as to the possibility of frail man's ability to influence physical conditions might have to be answered negatively.

But every atom of the body of the sick man is a powerhouse because it is indwelt by Universal Mind. Treatment releases this energy and lets it go to work. Man never stands alone in the universe. Always he is the embodiment of Power, which is ready to harmonize his whole being. Spiritual and mental healing is predicated upon this knowledge.

Man is part of the universe and one with his Maker. As Gray says in *The Advancing Front of Science:* "This curious, prying, stumbling, aspiring, peristently hopeful creature, man. Half brute that clings to the clod; half god who looks through distant light-years where the sun is shining."

It is this God-side of man that inspires us to believe that we have a right to expect the exercise of creative energy in healing. This is why we turn away from man as a physical organism and see him as a spiritual being when we are treating.

Each individual is eternally held as a perfect concept in Infinite Mind. This means that he is God's Perfect Idea. He has a right, therefore, to believe that Spirit desires perfect manifestation through him. This being so, there need be no hesitation upon his part in speaking his word for that perfection to be made manifest through him.

SOMETHING BETTER THAN HEALING

Healing is a blessed experience. But there is something better even than being healed. It is living in daily appreciation of the fact that we are perpetually indwelt by Spirit; that Mind is continuously operating in and through us.

The day will come when men do not use this healing Principle only when in difficulty, but when they will culti-

vate this sense of the Infinite nearness, its immanence, for
its own sake. When that day comes, sickness will be to the
race only a nightmare from which their ancestors suffered.
This truth is equivalent to a spiritual incoming of Power,
touching man first at his spiritual center, then spreading
out through his mentality to the physical envelope.

Man is never life in himself apart from God. Health,
prosperity, happiness, beautiful as they are, can never be
primary. They are always secondary. As the Presbyterian
Catechism says in answer to the question, "What is the
chief end of man?" it is "To glorify God and enjoy Him
forever." There must first be a sense of the Infinite indwelling; then all these things assume their rightful place. As
one learns to cultivate that sense of the Presence within,
these secondary blessings naturally manifest themselves.

To the person who thus lifts himself into higher levels
of thought and life, a new view of the world comes. He
sees the world groaning under defeat, sickness, and frustration; but he is deeply conscious of harmony and health.
He stands, as it were, upon the balcony of heaven and looks
down upon suffering humanity. He seems to live and move
in another world, lifted high above the false belief in the
necessity for sickness, and wishing that all men could see
and understand that disease is a reality only to those who
believe it is.

When he speaks his word for those who seek to be de-
livered from that bondage, his word has power because it is
alive with the consciousness of his oneness with Power.

"OFF THE DEEP END"

At this very moment, there is latent in every person enough of the power of God to transform him and lift him entirely out of his difficulty.

He may have been percussed and stethoscoped, fluoroscoped and X-rayed. He may have had blood count, blood chemistry, and basal metabolism tests. He may have had his blood pressure taken, and the body excretions analyzed. Then he may have been very gently informed that it is a great pity, but there is nothing that can be done.

That person should drop the diagnosis, ignore the prognosis, turn away from his terror, and say to himself:

"I know that all the Life of the universe streams through my body at this moment. I know that Mind knows nothing of such things as incurable conditions. I know that the only thing that hinders my complete restoration right now is my own blindness to truth.

"From this moment, I affirm my oneness with the Infinite Perfection. I drop my belief in the actuality of disease, and affirm my faith in the Perfect Presence within. I do not have to call to a far-distant God who sits in the heavens. The God of the universe is within me now. He has been there all my life, never forcing Himself upon me, but momentarily awaiting my recognition.

"All my life I have been blind, but now my eyes are open to the truth, and the truth sets me free from the law of sin and death.

"At this moment, I dwell upon the fact that the great creative Law of Mind awaits my word. I speak my word for the manifestation in me of all that Spirit is in itself.

"I give thanks for my uncovered perfection, and I release myself, lock, stock, and barrel, diagnosis, prognosis,
and feelings, to the creative activity of Mind."

Then he should turn away from the whole condition
with the thought, "Here I go, off the deep end, sink or
swim." The very fact of releasing one's entire condition
to Mind will help to relax him mentally so that no longer
does he interpose his own tenseness between himself and
the perfect working of Spirit through Mind.

This was the recommendation given many years ago to
a woman who consulted me. She had been given up by the
doctors after having had her case diagnosed as absolutely
hopeless. Years later, she reminded me of the "deep end"
treatment. "At that time," she said, "I actually felt that I
was diving in off the deep end, but I discovered that it was
the depths of Mind into which I plunged." She went a long
way after that day years ago, and became the means of
bringing many people to see and understand this truth.

One of the remarkable things about mental and spiritual
healings is that it can happen in a flash. One does not have
to study for years in order to be able to put it into practice.
True, some people take longer than others before the inward conviction is clear and strong; but one could take the
treatment set down above, and by opening himself up to it
without any mental reservations, he could be healed.

Once a person has experienced healing, it is natural that
he should want to go on and learn more. The reason for
this is that since he has opened wide his consciousness to
the recognition of the God within, Spirit within him continues to expand into larger and larger recognition. Something actual has happened. Healing is not merely a transfer

of thought; it is a movement of Spirit through the Law of Mind. Mind and body are changed. "Old things are passed away; behold, all things are new."

BACK TO THE FATHER'S HOUSE

Man has been a long time away from the Father's House, but now he is on his way back.

In the story of the prodigal son, Jesus was teaching how man brings his own miseries on himself. It was by no means a dissertation on morals. Jesus was never a moralist, as we have before indicated. He taught practical ways to change one's conditions.

The son wanted to leave the father's house, where all was peaceful and harmonious, and where he had only to make his wants known and they were amply supplied. The father did not argue with him, and he went away.

After a time, he found himself in dire straits and tried to figure out how he had managed to get into this condition. At last he saw light. His predicament was the result of separation from the father. He remembered how even the servants at home were fed, clothed, and kept happy. So he started home.

Getting there, he began to condemn himself to the father. But the father, who had not argued when he left, did not listen to his self-condemnation when he returned. Instead, he loved, fed, and clothed him, and the son dropped once more into his rightful place in the home.

The Father never changes: God is forever the Unchanging One. Man can do as he pleases with his life, for he is a free agent. But the Law of Cause and Effect ordains that he shall take the effect of his choices. Every move the son made was his own, conceived and executed by himself, without either urging or hindrance on the part of the father. The father was there when he left, and was in the same place when he came back.

The father's home was the place where there was common acceptance of the father's standards. In consequence, it was the place where man's highest security and happiness could be obtained. The far country was the world of opinions, where false beliefs prevailed, where the senses dominated, and where unhappiness and insecurity were the end of all action.

Man always recovers from the effect of his sense-life when he turns his mind inward to the Father's House. There is a place within the depths of man's consciousness that is the Father's House. It is that which was spoken of by the Psalmist when he said, "He that dwelleth in the secret place of the Most High shall abide under the shadow of the Almighty."

The world of the senses is a noisy place. The world of the Spirit is the place of peace. The world of the senses tears one to pieces. The world of the Spirit heals and integrates him.

It is man's privilege to close his ears to the raucous voices of the world of the senses, and penetrate deeper and deeper into the world of Reality which lies within.

One can imagine an underground tunnel in the heart of a great city. This tunnel leads for a considerable distance down, then gradually widens out into a huge room, where lights are soft and shaded, where soft rugs carpet the floor, where there are comfortable chairs and couches, and where the stillness can almost be felt.

The tired, distraught city-dweller turns from the noise and clangor of city streets, the ringing of traffic bells, the blare of automobile horns, the clatter of streetcars, the cries of newsboys. As he enters the tunnel, the noises are somewhat dimmed. The farther he makes his way, the less they beat upon his ears. Gradually, they drop to a whisper, and then, as he enters the room, they can no longer be heard, and he finds himself shut completely away from them.

This is the picture conveyed by the story of the prodigal son as he re-enters his father's house.

Most people continue to live amid the cacophony of the streets. Many, seeking Reality, withdraw a little way into the tunnel; the few make their way deep into the heart of Reality, where the aches, pains, and sicknesses of life cannot send up their discordant voices. These are they who dwell in the secret place of the Most High. Jesus lived this withdrawn life even in the midst of a busy outer practical life.

We do not have to be hermits, nor withdraw to cloisters or solitary mountaintops. We can carry on the multitudinous duties of this workaday world; yet the inner man can be forever in contact with the Father within. This is what is meant by "being in the world, yet not of it." The lily can live surrounded by the slime of the pond, but draw into itself those elements that emerge in a singular purity and beauty.

Dwell deep, my soul, dwell deep. This is the secret of peace.

Man must change: The currents of Life are always streaming in one direction. They will never change the course of their flow, just as the father never changed his position. Man must adapt himself to this flow of Life, in which case he finds complete harmony.

All of man's ills come from his crossing Life's currents. He can destroy himself by doing this. The destruction never comes from Spirit, but from the fact that man has stepped out and run counter to the universal harmonious flow.

Pleading and prayer will not cause the Father to change the direction of the stream of harmony. Man must return from the far country and drop once more into his rightful place, co-operating with, instead of striking across, the current. This is the true teaching of Cause and Effect.

Man is all Mind, from soul to physical atoms. Just as the thought of God, condensed down, became the actual physical universe, so the thought of man, condensed down, becomes his little physical universe. It is not strictly true to say that man's thought-life merely influences his physical life. We repeat it from time to time because it is a good way to draw attention to the power of thought. But the truth is that man's thought actually becomes his material form. Man's circumstances and his physical condition actually are his own thought-pattern molded into form.

This is why we say that his manifestation can never rise one inch above his thought level. His material conditions are always the index to his inner thought-life because they are that thought-life.

This is why the higher the quality of our thought, the

higher its effect. It is why we seek to draw the spiritual into our treatment.

The mysterious power of Spirit is higher than either physical or mental vibration. It is pure Spirit, immeasurably beyond mental power, concentration, suggestion, or any of the psychological activities. It is not registerable through the mere human faculties. It operates silently, as sunlight settles over the land.

For this reason, the treatment is not always registered through the senses, for the action is extra-sensory. During a treatment, the patient does not necessarily feel any different, and sometimes is disappointed that there is no sensation as of a fire entering him, or of some manifestation of something having happened to him.

Let him go his way, knowing that the Life of Spirit is not a tangible, electric thing, heralding its presence by a blare of emotional or physical trumpets. It steals silently throughout the body, actively operating in every cell, reproducing its own likeness wherever it is allowed recognition, doing all this with the same competent stillness with which its Intelligence runs the universe.

The effects are seen, however. The body thus operated upon by Spirit begins to show an improvement in outward conditions. A new stillness enters the consciousness, a new vitality begins to make itself apparent, the old order begins to pass away, and all things are made new.

THE RESISTLESSNESS OF THE INFINITE EXPRESSION

Life can never be restrained. It will always push its way to the surface. Nothing can stand in its way. Life in the tree roots will push the concrete sidewalk up, not in any explosive upheaval, but by the steady, sure drive of power that flows from the Source of all Life.

Life within the body of man, the Life of Spirit, will just as resistlessly eliminate the concrete slab of sickness or the constricting band of fear when it is contacted in this scientific manner.

Our responsibility: We must divest ourselves of all superstition, and know within ourselves that this Law of Life is not to be approached with fear and trembling. It is our Servant, and we may confidently direct it into action in the specific field upon which our choice has fallen.

Latent now, in each individual soul, is Infinite Power sufficient to transform his entire body into perfection. That Power is filtered through the human consciousness. There is no other way it can operate, for if God is to do anything for us, He has to do it through us. We may sit in the pigpen of a far country, commiserating ourselves, wondering why life has done this thing to us, and a loving Father will not lift a finger to bring us out of our misery. That is our responsibility.

As soon as we make up our mind to arise and go to the Father, we find that all the resources of the Father are at our disposal. We could have had them at any time, could have enjoyed them during the years we suffered in the far country, for they were all ours during the whole time. But we can never enjoy the actual possession of them until we, of our own volition, go back home and take them.

So we conclude our discussion with a clear, open-eyed awareness of the certainty of healing that is not dependent upon the uncertain whim of a heavenly Potentate, but which lies within our own power to take or to refuse. Those who refuse will find no other way to enter into complete physical freedom. Those who take will enter into the fullest measure of life, for "I am come that they might have life, and that they might have it more abundantly."

POINTS FOR SPECIAL CONSIDERATION

The reader who wants to become more aware of the perfectly natural connection between true religion and healing will give much thought to the ideas below.

The unbreakable unity of God in His universe is the basis of our work.

The highest thought that man can exercise is of God and perfection.

The great throbbing, pulsating Cosmic Energy is ours for the using.

When we are treating, we turn away from man as a physical organism and see him as a spiritual being.

Healing is a blessed experience. But there is something better even than being healed. It is living in daily appreciation of the fact that we are perpetually indwelt by Spirit, that Mind is continuously operating in and through us.

Healing is not dependent upon the uncertain whim of a heavenly Potentate, but lies within our power to take or to refuse.

Index